The Reason for the Seasons

James V. Schall, S.J.

The Reason
for the Seasons

Why Christians Celebrate What
and When They Do

SOPHIA INSTITUTE PRESS
Manchester, New Hampshire

Sophia Institute Press
Box 5284, Manchester, NH 03108
1-800-888-9344

www.SophiaInstitute.com

Sophia Institute Press® is a registered trademark of Sophia Institute.

Library of Congress Cataloging-in-Publication Data

Names: Schall, James V., author.
Title: The reason for the seasons : why Christians celebrate what and when
 they do / by James V. Schall, S.J.
Description: Manchester, New Hampshire : Sophia Institute Press, 2018. |
 Includes bibliographical references.
Identifiers: LCCN 2018037156 | ISBN 9781622826902 (pbk. : alk. paper)
Subjects: LCSH: Fasts and feasts—Catholic Church. | Church year. |
 Apologetics.
Classification: LCC BV30 . S3185 2018 | DDC 263—dc23 LC record available
at https://lccn.loc.gov/2018037156

First printing

To my sister, Norma Jean Vertin,
who, on holidays, filled our house
with the music of Christmas and Easter

So convinced were the ancients that wonder is something distinctively human that there was even an "argument from wonder" that was proffered as an argument in favor of the genuine humanity of Christ in the controversies surrounding Christological dogma.

—Josef Pieper, *For the Love of Wisdom*

No other story, no pagan legend or philosophical anecdote or historical event, does in fact affect us with that same peculiar and even poignant impression produced on us by the word *Bethlehem*. No other birth of a god or childhood of a sage seems to us to be Christmas or anything like Christmas.

—G. K. Chesterton, *The Everlasting Man*

On the 9th of April, being Good Friday, I, Boswell, break-fasted with Samuel Johnson on tea and cross-buns, Doctor Level making the tea. He carried me with him to the church of St. Clement Danes, where he had his seat, and his be-havior was, as I had imagined to myself, solemnly devout. I shall never forget the tremendous earnestness with which he pronounced the awful petition of the Litany: "In the hour of my death, and at the day of judgment, good Lord, deliver us." We went to church both in the morning and in the evening. In the interval between the two services we did not dine; but he read in the Greek New Testament.

—James Boswell, *The Life of Johnson*

You created Heaven and earth, but you did not make them of your own substance. If you had done so, they would have been equal to your only-begotten Son, and therefore to yourself, and justice could in no way admit that what was not of your own substance should be equal to you. But besides yourself, O God, who are Trinity in Unity, Unity in Trinity, there was nothing from which you could make Heaven and earth.

—St. Augustine, *Confessions*

And yet we cannot avoid the appalling realization, that at no time have the revolt from Christ and the supernatural and the idealization of man and his nature been so noisily proclaimed, so audaciously organized and carried into effect with such terrible severity and such extensive display of power as in these days in which we live. The era of the serpent is near. Already its word, "Ye shall be as gods," may be heard in the streets and lanes. Did Christ die in vain?... Because man is inexhaustible in his wickedness, God must be inexhaustible in His redemptive love, that He will subdue such wickedness by the superabundance of His love.

—Karl Adam, *The Son of God*

Contents

Part 2
From Ash Wednesday to Easter

Part 3

From the Ascension to Pentecost

Part 4

Ordinary Time

Part 5

From All Saints to the Immaculate Conception

Acknowledgments

The author wishes to thank the publishers and editors of the following sources for permission to reprint these essays: *The Catholic Thing, Catholic World Report, Gilbert Magazine, Crisis Magazine, MercatorNet, Aleteia.org, The Hoya, National Review, Inside Catholic,* and *The University Bookman*.

The Reason for the Seasons

Introduction

Over the years, I have written a number of relatively short essays on various Church feasts. These feasts are always an occasion to ask: "What is the point of the celebration?" "Why is it a case, not just of rejoicing, but of knowing the truth that makes real joy possible?" We cannot be joyful without ultimately knowing why we should be joyful, without having something to be joyful about.

In particular, I have written (and include here) many reflections on Christmas, Easter, and the days surrounding them. Also in this text are considerations of Pentecost, All Saints' Day, and All Souls' Day as well as of the "End Times" that come up in the last Sundays of the Liturgical Year.

I have also included my 2009 essay on Msgr. Robert Hugh Benson's novel *The Lord of the World*, because the book now has been cited any number of times by Pope Francis. It fits in with the Gospel themes for the last days of the Liturgical Year, when we are reminded of the end of our temporal existence.

The feast of the Immaculate Conception, which is the transition to the Nativity cycle, completes the Liturgical Year. I do not talk much here of Advent, Lent, or the various other celebrations of the Lord or of the saints. Although these seasons are important, I want to focus in these pages on more central considerations.

It has always been a pleasure and an inspiration for me to say something each year on Christmas and Easter. These days are never-ending causes of insight into what we are and who God is. For that reason, you need not sit down and read this book from page 1 to its end, although there is nothing wrong in doing so. Each chapter is its own reflection. Come back to the same feast again and again: each time you will find something astonishingly new that you missed before.

These essays are not homilies or sermons, though they can be made into them. Rather, they are each intended to reveal something of the meaning and depth of the occasion that we might otherwise pass over unnoticed.

All Christian feasts have in common their particularity in time and place as well as their transcendent reaching to the truth that God has revealed to us. The second reading of each day in the Breviary, for instance, can come from any time or place in the past two thousand years and still speak to us as we read it.

Likewise, although they speak of universals, sometimes these essays reflect the time in which they were written, so I have included on the first page of each chapter the source and date of its first publication.

The reader will notice that I have my favorite authors and books. No one writes better about Christmas than Chesterton. Anyone who reads the Breviary knows that its readings contain a wealth of information and insight along with their prayerful nature.

In our day, the basic truths of Christianity are not well known. They are often rejected before their point or reasonableness is seen. Rejection of the truths of faith and reason is not always,

Introduction

or even mostly, due to lack of intelligence or diligence. They are rejected because people do not want them to be true, as their truth would affect the way people live. So people blind themselves to their logic and evidence. They formulate theories or ideologies that claim to be the real world, when actually they are subjective projections onto reality that do not correspond to it.

The Liturgical Year is composed of an Advent season, a Christmas season, a Lenten season, an Easter season that ends with Pentecost, and a remaining season of Ordinary Time that constitutes generally the periods from the end of the Christmas season to the beginning of Lent and from Pentecost to the beginning of Advent. Each day of the year has its own special atmosphere and Liturgy, either of the season or the day. Often, we find more than one feast on the same day. Here, I spend much time on Christmas and Easter, because they not only commemorate the principal truths of the Faith but also, as such, offer an enormous opportunity to think about what is handed down to us. Indeed, revelation was given to us, among other reasons, precisely so that we would think more clearly.

As I noted earlier, you will find here several chapters on Christmas, Easter, Pentecost, All Souls' Day, and the End Times. These chapters are not intended to be a comprehensive discussion of the feast in question, but they reveal strikingly different things we can learn about each of them every time we celebrate or encounter them.

Each feast — each separate consideration of a feast — is something "to be wondered about." And we do not "wonder" for wonder's sake, but to find the truth of what we wonder about. Simply to wonder with no hope of finding the truth is bewildering. Aristotle, the man who told us that philosophy begins in wonder, was the same man who answered many of his initial wonderments.

5

The Reason for the Seasons

The events and the occasions that feasts commemorate in their own right have the same effect on us. They cause us not only to wonder but to find the truth as a result of our inquiry and longing. The spirit of these reflections on the great feasts is one of awe, but of an awe that is fully aware of the truth that makes us free.

Part 1

From Christmas to New Year's

Chapter 1

⁀

Who Made Christmas?[1]

One writer against Christmas went so far as to say that the shopkeepers for their own commercial purposes alone sustain Christmas Day. I am not sure whether he said that the shop- keepers invented Christmas Day. Perhaps he thought that the shopkeepers invented Christianity. It is a quaint picture, the secret conclave between the cheese-monger, the poulterer, and the toy-shop keeper, in order to draw up a theology that shall convert all Europe and sell some of their goods. That the shopkeepers make Christmas is about as conceivable as that the confectioners make children. It is about as sane as that milliners manufacture women.

—G.K. Chesterton, *Illustrated London News*, January 13, 1906

Over a century ago at Christmastide, with no little amusement, Chesterton attacked the central heresy: Did commercial Christ- mas invent this memorable feast, or did Christmas come first, with commercialism later, as a prosperous afterthought? The idea that commercial folks could get together in a back room to dream up a theology explaining the core idea of Christmas, then proceed to convince the world of its truth—all so that the

[1] Published online, *National Review*, December 22, 2005.

9

merchants could make a bundle of money during the otherwise dull winter solstice — is, on the face of it, absurd.

Shopkeepers did not, in their greed or entrepreneurship, dream up Christmas. Neither did theologians. It is the other way around. Christmas, being what it is — a gift of no merely human origin — is a boon to shopkeepers and a stimulus to theologians. It is closer to the truth to say that Christmas invented shopkeepers and theologians than it is to say that shopkeepers and theologians manufactured Christianity. Shopkeepers antedated Christianity. In Africa and Asia today, shopkeepers are most likely to be Hindus or Arabs or Chinese. Shopkeepers did not need Christianity to be shopkeepers. It seems less clear, however, whether theologians could exist without Christianity.

No theologian could invent Christmas from the fervid ponderings of his own mind. Too few in this guild can, in fact, even accurately explain what Christmas is about, even though it was not invented by them. Many opponents of Christianity "would believe anything except Christianity." That is, many would do anything but understand what exactly it is that constitutes the precise explication of Christmas.

Some relation does exist between what we understand Christmas to be and how festively we celebrate it — or how inappropriately we celebrate it or even refuse to celebrate it. Christmas customs and traditions should exist in order to explain more profoundly what the feast is about. Too often, however, they obscure its meaning. Unless they are inspired by the truth of this feast and lead back to it, customs can, if we are not careful, lead us away from the heart of Christmas.

A former student was in town. An American, she married a Spaniard and has a daughter. Their family spent time in Switzerland. She laughed that one year her daughter had three

Who Made Christmas?

"Christmases" — St. Nicholas Day in Switzerland, Christmas Day in Philadelphia, and the feast of the Three Kings in Spain. These are all gift-giving and gift-receiving days.

The American Christmas, like its population, is a collection and mixture, even a hodgepodge, of Christmas traditions from all over the world rolled into one. We add our own touches with Bing Crosby's "White Christmas," the ubiquitous and improbable Rudolph, and "All I Want for Christmas Is My Two Front Teeth."

The Mexican tradition of lighted candles in sand-filled bags to guide the Holy Family to our homes is found in our Southwest. We all have, brightened with the latest technology, German Christmas trees, when we do not have artificial ones made in China. Some have English Yule logs. Chesterton thought that our modern Christmas mood was largely the invention of Dickens. Santa Claus, though himself from Bari in Italy via a town in Turkey, has Scandinavian origins. Some reactionary people actually have mangers and cribs. I was once in Oberammergau in Bavaria, where they produce wonderful wood carvings of the Nativity scenes sold all over the world.

Some purists want only such Nativity scenes, no pagan greenery. Likewise, we find ideologues who want anything but Nativity scenes, especially where they will be seen. The early Puritans in New England forbade Christmas. Today, greeting someone with a cheery "Merry Christmas" is said to violate your neighbor's constitutional right to your silence. Some do not want to be reminded of the day's meaning. We all have experienced the madness of substituting "holiday" parties for "Christmas" parties. I refuse to go to anything called a "holiday" party during the Christmas season. Yes, I miss a lot of parties!

School systems have taken the lead in driving out any reference to Christmas, even its name. "Winter," not "Christmas," breaks are in order. We fear not only the idea of Christmas, but the very word *Christmas*. I sometimes suspect there is more here than meets the eye. It is not just a question of keeping us from "imposing" Christmas on others, but the unsettling sense that the joy that is connected with this feast cannot even be admitted to exist. If Christmas is not a natural "right" for everyone of whatever persuasion, it must be prohibited as a private privilege for anyone.

At bottom, however, Christmas cannot be held or enjoyed except on its own terms; that is, except on condition of acknowledging what we celebrate. Christmas not only means that a Child is born unto us, but that, because of this birth, this world is not sufficient to us, not our final home. And Christmas is the feast of the home, both our family home and our eternal home. Aside from Plato's *Republic*, we live in the first age in the history of the world that questions the proper makeup of a home (with husband, wife, and children); and actually engineers or legislates alternatives to it.

* * *

Roughly, there are two contrary traditions about Christmas and how properly to celebrate it. One is the "expectation" approach, the waiting for something to happen, the longing for the real explanation of *what we are*. This season in the Church is called Advent. It recalls the long preparation for the coming of Christ that we see in the Old Testament. Isaiah 25:6 proclaims that "On this mountain the LORD of hosts will provide for all peoples a feast of rich food and choice wines: juicy, rich food and pure, choice wines." These are menus we Christians anticipate for Christmas.

We renew this mood and atmosphere of anticipation in the month before Christmas. If a person does not expect such a thing from the Old Testament, Christmas, as Christians know it, must seem like an illusion. Christians, however, hold that solid textual, historical, and theoretical foundations exist for what they maintain about the birth of Christ in Bethlehem: who He was, where He came from, both His far-reaching origins in a Jewish family and His transcendent origin as the Word now made flesh, the Son of God, to dwell amongst us.

The "anticipation" approach is one of expectation, of a hushness over the world, even of penance. Advent contains a sense both of our unworthiness and of our longings. *Veni, veni, Emmanuel, captivum solve Israel* (O come, O come, Emmanuel, and ransom captive Israel).

Preparations for Christmas begin to be seen in the streets and shops around Thanksgiving in this country. Even in towns and cities that insist on paganism in decorations, whose public squares are truly naked, with only lights, greens, and tinsel, no crèches, no angels singing on high, it is difficult to avoid the impression that something not yet here is coming in the stillness of the night, in the "Silent Night, Holy Night." Indeed, in areas where Nativity scenes are still allowed, or in homes and churches that have them, the full manger scene with Joseph, Mary, the Child, and the shepherds does not appear until Christmas Eve.

In most cities, a radio station or two are still free to play well-known and not-so-well-known Christmas music from the classic traditions to those of various ethnic origins, and even liturgical music. It is not uncommon to find among the best sellers CDs or other forms of recorded music, all performed by the finest orchestras and vocalists. And if one likes bluegrass or country-and-western music, stations specializing in it are sometimes very good at keeping, playing, and indeed composing Christmas music. It may be easier to drive the Christ Child out of the public square than out of the airwaves.

Plans are made, presents bought, cards sent, homes decorated. Students come home; relatives plan to meet. Christmas is a season for food and drink, eggnog, wassail. Traditions and memories are kept alive by the smell of mincemeat pie, turkey, popcorn balls, and "chestnuts roasting on an open fire." Reds and greens appear in our garb.

Behind all of these preparations lies the expectation, the sense of something being given to us, something intended for us but about which we have no control. We are not worthy. It is a gift, not a reward, not something earned. Yet it comes because we sense something lacking in us. We wait. No real appreciation of something can exist unless we also wait for it, wait in some awe.

The second tradition is what I might call the "celebration" tradition: the Twelve Days of Christmas, the days from Christmas to the feast of the Magi, the Three Kings, in January, with the feasts of Stephen, of the Holy Innocents, Becket, good King Wenceslaus, and St. Sylvester in between, and with a rather secular New Year's Day being thrown in for good measure. The dating of Christmas does seem to have something to do with supplanting pagan feasts, but also, as Chesterton said, with keeping what is best in the pagan traditions.

Like any birthday of any given human being, Christmas, the birth of one of our kind, cannot be fathomed in one day. Yet its own day — Christmas Day — is the best day. A celebration is what we do when something beyond our powers or sometimes even beyond our comprehension happens to us, something that is addressed to the heart of things, to our very meaning, to our very souls.

Who Made Christmas?

* * *

Both the anticipation and the celebration are essential to Christmas. Joseph and Mary were in Bethlehem because of a "decree that went out from Caesar Augustus" (Luke 2:1). How remarkable in Luke's Gospel is this "coincidence," this linking of the first Roman emperor with the birth in a manger of the Son of Man, in that particular place at the origins of the House of David. But few knew of this event when it happened. Although angels were singing on high, it was a while before any Roman historians even hinted at it. Christmas is not a feast of great events in this world. Rather, it is a feast that reminds us that great things take place in small towns, in out-of-the-way places, things that need time to grow, to flourish.

Christmas somehow brings out in some people a kind of venom that strikes us Christians as bordering on the diabolical. "Why is this most tender of feasts subject to such resentment?" we wonder to ourselves. In these days of intolerant tolerance, we hesitate to speculate. We know of the words spoken of this Child born amongst us that many would rise and fall because of Him (see Luke 2:34). A sword would pierce the heart of His mother. He could not be ignored, even if rejected, perhaps especially if rejected. Such things go against the mood of our age, yet are truer in our age than ever before.

In the Breviary for Christmas Eve, a sermon of the great Augustine begins: "Awake, mankind! For your sake God has become man.... I tell you again: for your sake, God became man."

Is this the clue we need?

"You would have suffered eternal death, had He not been born in time. Never would you have been freed from sinful flesh, had He not taken on himself the likeness of sinful flesh." We do not like to be reminded of our sinfulness. We do not

15

like to know what is wrong, so that we are left free to do what we will.

On Christmas Eve, our redemption is at hand. Yet, it does not work itself out as we would have done it if we were in charge. The shadow of the Cross falls over the manger. It happens for "our sake." We are to be "awake," almost as if it is possible for us to miss this momentous thing that has happened to our kind. We can, indeed, choose not to see.

About Christmas, an incredible concreteness is found. Little things must be done for ordinary people, by ordinary people, ourselves included. John says in his first letter, "This is what we proclaim to you, what was from the beginning, what we have heard, what we have seen with our eyes, what we have looked upon and our hands have touched—we speak of the word of life" (see 1 John 1:1–2). Shopkeepers did not invent Christmas. Neither did the theologians.

We most associate Christmas with a gift. A gift is not something we can demand, not something that is due to us. Ultimately, the structure of the universe is first to be understood as a gift. Who made Christmas? "The Word was made flesh, and dwelt among us" (John 1:14, KJV).

It has never been put more succinctly. We can choose other explanations. No doubt many do. All gifts must be freely received by those to whom they are freely given. This is the principle upon which the universe is constructed.

Chapter 2

≈

On Hilarity and the Keeping of Christmas[2]

In *Heretics*, Chesterton briefly commented on Christmas. He announced that in this joyful season, he needed to "touch upon a very sad matter." This sad matter referred to those men in the modern world "who really make a protest on behalf of that *antiqua pulchritude* (ancient beauty) of which Augustine spoke. They "long for the old feasts and formalities of the childhood of the world."

Some Irishmen seek not the Christian but the pagan Irish customs and dances. Other people, presumably not Irish, want to restore the Maypoles and the original Olympic Games. *Heretics* was written in 1905. The first modern Olympic games were held in 1896.

Chesterton thought that these same people — he cited Yeats and George Moore — wanted to retrieve ancient festivals but that they "just possibly do not keep Christmas." They do not look up to see that a feast was being celebrated in the streets about them. The people who wanted Maypoles, Olympic discus throws, and pagan Celtic dances did not observe that Christmas

---

[2] Published in the *Midwest Chesterton News*, 1994.

trees were in the windows of ordinary folks. They did not wave their "spoons and shout when the pudding is set alight." The people, who now prattle on about ancient dances and games, had they been alive at their inception, would have considered the Canterbury pilgrimage and Olympic wrestling too vulgar for their tastes.

In fact, these events of celebration, like Christmas, were "vulgar." The Latin word *vulgus* means "the common, ordinary people." Christmas feasts were things of the people and not just ruminations of ascetics looking back nostalgically on some past they would never have themselves participated in if they were given a chance. Now, if a thing is popular or vulgar, Chesterton admitted, we should not doubt what this means: "Let no man deceive himself. If by vulgarity we mean coarseness of speech, rowdiness of behavior, gossip, horseplay, and some heavy drinking, vulgarity there always was whenever there was joy, whenever there was faith in the gods. Wherever you have belief you will have hilarity; wherever you have hilarity you will have some dangers."

These lines are remarkable. Belief leads to joy. Hilarity implies some risk. We can praise ancient dances because we will never be asked to dance them. But if we are at a feast that is grounded in faith, dancing and hence joy, and hence, if all join in, some hilarity, some vulgarity, and yes, some "heavy drinking" will possibly appear. Without the risk of freedom, there is no divine joy.

The erroneous conclusion is that, because of the dangers of vulgarity, of commonness, something is wrong with the dancing, with the joy, with the faith, with the drinking even. In this view, faith is not meant for everyone in his actual condition. This conclusion is the opposite of the truth.

On Hilarity and the Keeping of Christmas

We are joyful. We experience a sense of hilarity because the faith is true. We dance, sing, laugh, and are rowdy because we discover that the risk of God in creating and redeeming all of us was worthy of Him.

Christ became man in an obscure town, of quite unknown parents, in an odd corner of the Roman Empire. He was born in Bethlehem because Caesar Augustus, the emperor of the far-off Romans who ruled the place, ordered a census to be taken. Everyone—the *vulgus*—was to return to his town of origin to register. This unlikely census applied to Joseph and Mary. Christ was thus not born in the palaces of the Caesars. He was not even born among the high priests of the Jews or among the Magi. And yet, it is of His birth that we sing "Joy to the World." It is not just any "belief" that can cause "hilarity" but only a belief in the birth of the Son of God, who dwelt amongst us.

Christianity is a revelation not to the few but to the many, to everyone: to everyone, whether he knows it or not, whether he likes it or not. The few know how to respond to delight in a sophisticated way. The vulgar, the common, do not. But they do respond—with rough rowdiness, with gossip, with horseplay, with coarseness of speech. They do not know how to respond otherwise. But we are not to think that because of their vulgar manners and ways of expressing things that that over which they rejoice and delight does not exist. They are the ones who wave their spoons and shout when the plum pudding is lighted because they are the very ones who realize the risk that God took in dwelling amongst us.

The words of the angel to the shepherds in the infancy narrative in Luke's Gospel are always haunting to me. These shepherds, these vulgar, common folk, were terrified at what they saw and heard. In this regard, I cite the words of the King James Version:

And, lo, the angel of the Lord came upon them, and the glory of the Lord shone round about them: and they were sore afraid. And the angel said unto them, "Fear not: for behold, I bring you good tidings of great joy, which shall be to all people. For unto you is born this day in the city of David a Savior, which is Christ the Lord" (Luke 2:9–11).

This feast, which we still celebrate, is brought first to whom? The good tidings are of "great joy." They come to the shepherds and thence "to all people." The text does not say "unto Joseph and Mary" is born a Savior. It says that He is born unto the shepherds and to all the people.

We should note too that what is born this day in the city of David is not an idea. It is not a political movement. It is not a formula of physics. What is born is a particular Child, "which is Christ the Lord." The Word, we are told, was made flesh and dwelt amongst us. We are the "us" amongst whom the Lord dwelt and still dwells. Chesterton's exegesis on the dangers of vulgarity reminds us that this Incarnation and Nativity into the world is not an abstraction. Nor is it meant for only a few; nor are the elite few even likely to appreciate what happened in the city of David as well as do such folks as shepherds, "sore afraid," and delightful youngsters whose eyes open wide when the pudding is alight.

The fact that God accepted the danger of the reactions of common folks to His intervention reveals much about God. The risk of God, so to speak — and one that we encounter again at every Christmas — is that we will remain unmoved, dull, unperceptive about the greatest event in the history of our kind, which occurred in a little out-of-the-way place because of that decree of Caesar Augustus.

On Hilarity and the Keeping of Christmas

If we were God (Chesterton seems to say apropos of those who would not recognize real feasts if they saw them), we would have figured out a more dramatic and elevated way to dwell amongst us. We would have given no occasion for rowdiness or hilarity among the vulgar and common folks, the shepherds, the folks who dance and sing.

Wherever you have belief, you will have hilarity.

The *antiqua pulcritude* of Augustine, that beauty ever ancient, ever new: this is what came to dwell amongst us. In this joy, in this delight, we do not forget the Celtic dances or the discus throwers, any less than the shepherds and those among whom you might see some "heavy drinking."

For unto you is born this day in the city of David a Savior, which is Christ the Lord.

Chapter 3

≈

The Nativity of Christ: Its Historic Reality[3]

*How can we talk about God today? The first answer is that
we can talk about God because He has talked to us, so the first
condition for speaking of God is listening to all that God himself
has said. God has spoken to us! God is therefore not a distant
hypothesis concerning the world's origin; He is not a mathemati-
cal intelligence far from us. God takes an interest in us; He loves
us; He has entered personally into the reality of our history; He
has communicated himself, even to the point of taking flesh.*

—Pope Benedict XVI, Audience, November 28, 2012

A "War on Christmas" goes on in this and other countries. People are offended that even the mention of Christ's birth is found
in the public order. Great strides have been made to eliminate
any specific, public references to Christ and His birth—no Nativity scenes, no reference to Christmas but tinsel, secularized
songs, greenery, and various glittering things that refer to nothing really. Some allowance seems still to be made for Christmas
music, both the religious and the sentimental kinds. Much of it
is too beautiful to ignore.

[3] Published in *The Catholic Pulse*, December 23, 2013.

The Reason for the Seasons

A legal holiday is kept, not a birthday. We are admonished to be careful about wishing "Merry Christmas" to unknown souls. It is a one-way street, of course; we are to be concerned with the sensibilities of others, but they need not concern themselves much about ours. Religious freedom now means "Keep it quiet, whatever it is you hold. If you say nothing or do nothing about your beliefs, we will let you play with us."

We ought to know, however, just what this Nativity that we call Christmas really means. The history of much modern "critical" thought has been designed to deny (a) that Jesus existed and (b) that scriptural accounts are credible. Christmas is judged to be a myth.

The story of the Incarnation and birth of a god is the common stuff of many religions. Yet, with all this in mind, we are really rather astonished at the coherence of the Nativity account and what it means. The fact is that after centuries of trying to cast doubt on the reality of Christ's Incarnation into this world, we must say that all the evidence, when carefully examined, indicates that Christ lived in a definite time and place. He was who He said He was. No other explanation suffices to account for the evidence. The effort to show that Christ was unreal or something else has failed.

This fact does not mean that everyone will suddenly grant the truth of the Nativity event. For the most part, efforts to show that Christ did not exist or that reports of His life are unreliable were always grounded in the first place in a will not to believe the fact. This voluntary rejection is what led to the searches for reasons why Christ was not what He said He was. These searches sought to prove what the investigator wanted to be true. The truth of Christ's reality did not have to be taken into account.

The Nativity of Christ: Its Historic Reality

Most people saw clearly that, if the accounts of Christ's life and the understanding that He was indeed the Son of God now present in the history of this world were true, mankind would have to take this fact into its understanding of what man's purpose was.

And why was Christ born into this world? Our minds seek a reason to explain the fact. William of St. Thierry (d. 1148) put it well:

> And this is clearly the reason why You (God) first loved us so that we might love You—not because You needed our love, but because we could not be what You created us to be, except by loving you. In many ways and on various occasions you spoke to our fathers through the prophets. Now in these last days You have spoken to us in Your Son, Your Word. By Him the heavens were established, and all their powers came to be by the breath of His mouth.

This Word was made flesh and has spoken to us. We are addressed in our rational being. We are asked to understand. We exist because of nothing in ourselves. We are a gift unto ourselves. We exist in abundance and astonishment.

It is said that most people reject Christianity, not because they doubt the existence of an origin, of a God, but because of the claim that God, within His being, has an inner life. The only-begotten Son, the Image of the Father, becomes man. How could this be? Yet, if we look carefully at the explication of William of St. Thierry we see the answer. God did not have to create the heavens and the earth. Why did He do it then? In order that beings that were not God could also love God.

And when it was clear that God's plan for mankind was rejected by free men, God responded.

How?

Gently. The Father sent His Son to dwell amongst us.

Where?

He was born in Bethlehem of Judea.

When?

During the time of Caesar Augustus.

Why?

In order that we might be able to achieve the purpose for which we were created. God will not coerce us. We have to choose to see the reality of what occurred.

Why did this plan of God result in the Word becoming flesh? God might perhaps have redeemed us in some other way. But the way He chose was via the Nativity. A real Divine Person, now true God and true man, appeared amongst us so that we could freely respond to God's love of us when we saw the consequences of our rejecting Him.

Could God have done anything more than He did?

Undoubtedly, no.

Where does this leave us?

It leaves us at the scene of the Nativity.

What do we see there through the testimony of those who have passed on to us the account of Christ's birth in the manger?

We see Him through whom the world was created now entering this same world.

What is the conclusion?

The only sensible conclusion is that the world is simply not the same as it was before this event in Bethlehem. The history of the world changes at this point. Without understanding what happened here, we cannot understand ourselves. And this is what is happening to us as we remove all signs of the Nativity from our eyes and our souls. We find ourselves incapable of understanding ourselves. This is why the modern world is a world filled with human beings incapable of explaining themselves to themselves, but refusing to admit it. The name given to the Child at His Birth was Emmanuel, "God with us." It is still the name that best tells us what, during the reign of Caesar Augustus, the Nativity was about.

Chapter 4

⁀

Christmas Comes But Once a Year[4]

The famous Christmas carol begins: *Adeste fideles, laeti trium-phantes*. Few refrains are more haunting. The translation reads, "O come, all ye faithful, joyful and triumphant." The Latin is more succinct: "Come, be present, happy, and triumphant."

But, we wonder, be present where?

The answer comes: *Venite, venite in Bethlehem*. Come, come to Bethlehem.

We cannot come to Bethlehem. It is a distant, war-torn place, at the heart of the most troubled area of our time. Yet it remains a place to which, even now, we are "commanded" or "invited" to "come." Evidently, our time and place matter not. Once *He who is to come* has come, He is ever in our midst.

Why are we asked to "come" to Bethlehem? What is triumphant there?

A "triumph" was a Roman public celebration for a successful victory, a reward of honor. Why should Bethlehem engender happiness in us? The answer is forthcoming: *Natum videte Regem Angelorum*. In this place and time is "born" the "King of angels."

[4] Published in *Crisis Magazine*, December 2006.

Angels are not "born." Yet they have a "King" who evidently is. In what condition is this King?

He is a newborn. We see a baby, a child. We ask ourselves again: "Is He really a child, but also the King of angels?" This is rather much. A child is the King of angels?

What is this verb, *videte*? What are we to do on arrival there? Are we only there to "see" Him? This is about all we can do to any baby, after all. We are indeed ordered to "see" Him. "See the one who is born." The first wonder consists in seeing what has been born to us, that such a Child could be at all. Initially, we know only that He exists.

"But why is it," we wonder, "that the hymn sounds so much better sung?" If we just memorized the words, but not the music, would we remember it at all? It is no accident that music takes words beyond themselves.

Each stanza to the hymn is followed by a chorus: *Venite, adoremus*. Literally this reads, "Come, let us adore." In English, we sing, "Let us adore Him." The operative verb is "adore." This "adoration" harkens back to the title He is given: "King of angels." We do not "adore" angels. The verb *adorare* is specific. We ought not "adore" just anybody or anything. We are warned about idolatry. "To adore" is reserved for a relation to whom and to what this "King of angels" really is. If He is not "divine," we ought not to adore Him.

The refrain continue: *Venite, adoremus*. The words are repeated. "Come, adore. Let us adore." Repetition is often the best thing we can do before what is glorious. The Latin finally gives us the "object" of this "adoration." *Dominum*. The Lord is Christ, the Child in Bethlehem. This is the Incarnation, the most difficult of all Christian doctrines to believe, even more so than the Trinity.

This famous hymn was written by an Englishman, John Francis Wade, in about 1760. Wade was a Catholic layman, a music teacher, who fled English persecution to Douai, the famous English college in France. The hymn was originally written in Latin, but soon had an English translation.

The sixth and last stanza of this hymn sings: "Yea, Lord, we greet Thee, born this happy morning. Jesus, to Thee be glory given; Word of the Father, now in the flesh appearing."

I have always loved phrases that begin: "Yea, Lord." The theology is correct. Jesus is the Word of the Father, the Logos, now appearing in the flesh. We do not "greet" Jesus just because He is another man, however wonderful that be. He is more than that.

Christmas morning is "happy" not because it is another morning but because it is "this happy morning." We now have someone amongst us to whom "glory" is to be given. This is all we can do, give "glory," acknowledge *what is*.

But present at His birth were His mother, Joseph, soon also the shepherds from the fields, and the Magi from the East.

From the Magi, word reached Herod that something might threaten his reign, a "King of angels," no less. So Herod set about seeking to kill Him. In the process, he killed male children from the neighborhood—the "holy" innocents, who still witness to all wanton killing of children, in or outside the womb. Others would later succeed in killing Jesus, where Herod failed.

Venite, adoremus, Venite adoremus Dominum.

Chapter 5

"Here's Wishing You a Merry Christmas"[5]

A colleague mentioned hearing "White Christmas" or "Here's Wishing You a Merry Christmas" in Japanese during Christmastide. This is seasonal music popular among those who generally do not believe in what Christmas stands for. Similarly, during my European years, I was struck by the different cultural expressions surrounding Christmas among those who did historically hold it. My Australian friends celebrate Christmas during the height of summer, a practice that makes our external symbols — snow, ice, bare trees — seem irrelevant. The early American Puritans suppressed Christmas on anti-papist grounds. Just what Christmas might mean in a Muslim culture, where its doctrine is heresy, or in a Hindu world, is anybody's guess.

I have always liked "White Christmas." But clearly, "White Christmas," even with Bing Crosby, is a deflection from what Christmas is. It is a confusion of atmosphere with substance. We now think twice about wishing our neighbor "Merry Christmas" lest we "impose" our beliefs on the poor man. Whatever it is that our heads are full of, we do not want anyone to find out lest he

<hr>

[5] Published in *Crisis Magazine*, December 2004.

be upset by a real idea. The ultimate defense against truth is the refusal to know.

"Adeste Fideles" is glorious and memorable. But one is hard-pressed to imagine what these words and music might mean to someone theologically clueless or metaphysically antagonistic to the truths contained in the hymn. I can, to some extent, enjoy a Wagner opera without following the German, but, as with "Adeste Fideles," I should know what it means.

Any great theological truth or any event as great as the birth of Christ causes profound and unending reflection on what it means. We can express our understanding in terms of poetry, music, dance, essays, treatises, or hymns. Truth breeds truth, along with multiple ways of expressing it or coming to terms with it.

Christmas in the United States in recent years is being driven indoors. Someone is ever "offended" by any public display of it. The reason for offense is that Christmas is a doctrine proposed to be true, not just that the music celebrating it is beautiful. We did not make its truth up. What Christmas is remains true whether we succeed in expressing it culturally or not, though it is our natural thrust to embody it in diverse ways.

Christmas is, of course, the great family feast that, as Chesterton said, should be celebrated indoors, with those we love and those who love us. But we come back to the question: "What does Christmas mean?" We should not lose this understanding contained in the tradition or refuse to face its implications because we do not want to hear it.

Christmas is a truth about God. Its initiative does not come from man.

Briefly, it affirms that the world did not make itself to be what it is. Before the world is "I AM" (Exod. 3:14). It turns out that the Godhead has its own proper inner life, complete in itself, having no need of the world or us.

However, for His own purposes, God created the world, within which and for His purposes exists a central, free creature, the human being. This being, each of its existing members in time, is intended to participate in the inner life of God. God created a world in which He could be rejected by the free creature. He was, in fact, rejected.

God's response to this rejection was to send into the world His Son, the Eternal Word, who was born of Mary in Bethlehem during the reign of Caesar Augustus. This Incarnation, as it is called, this birth, life, and death of Christ, is the central event of human history and explains it. When we celebrate Christmas, this is what we celebrate, that Christ is true God and true man.

Understanding this, everything else makes sense.

Not understanding it, little else does.

Chapter 6

≈

Grace Revealed[6]

The readings from Paul during Christmastide do not contain vivid scenes of a crib, donkeys, and shepherds. We do not hear angels singing on high, or see the Holy Family, the Inn, or Magi pulling up their camels. Paul wasn't around Bethlehem at the time. What we do hear is his explanation of what Christmas is ultimately about. Since it has been largely abolished from our public order, "What is Christmas?" needs frequent articulation.

At one time, I thought that the neglect of Christmas was due to lethargy. I no longer think this. In many ways that we do not admit even to ourselves, Christmas is hated and plotted against for what it technically is. We need to be frank about this.

In the depths of the Godhead, however, Christmas is intended for everyone. Its truth is that the Second Person of the Trinity was made flesh. He did dwell amongst us. Once this happened, the world is different. It must accept or reject its relation to this event.

I have always liked the sentimental songs of Christmas — "Chestnuts Roasting on an Open Fire," "White Christmas," and

6   Published in *The Catholic Thing*, December 23, 2009.

37

The Reason for the Seasons

"I'll Have a Blue Christmas without You." I can even tolerate "Rudolph the Red-Nosed Reindeer" and "Jingle Bells," but not the "Sleigh Bells Jingling" song. Even though crib scenes are now private, Christmas trees still retain some more-than-secular meaning. Yet the other day, in the CVS store down on Wisconsin Avenue, I found for sale not a single Christmas card depicting the real Christmas—only Santas, fir trees, snow, ribbons, and birdies in various poses.

From the Christmas Masses, my favorite text that explains what Christmas is about is the second reading from the Midnight Mass, from Paul's second chapter of Titus. The text begins: "God's grace has been revealed." What startling words! Obviously, what is "revealed" refers to the birth of Christ, not to some abstraction. What we see is not "grace" but the Child in the manger. This "grace" that we now behold was not "revealed" before this moment. Something new has happened in our world.

What has this "grace" done? It made "salvation possible for the whole human race." The event is not just for members of the family of Mary and Joseph, or even for Israel itself. How is it that we can say of this Child, as of no other child, that, because of Him, "salvation" for each of us—each human being—is now "possible"?

We are next taught something more sober. We are to "give up everything that does not lead to God." Is there anything that does not "lead to God"? In principle, no. But we are to give up our ambitious, "worldly" use of things that lead only to ourselves.

"We must be self-restrained and live good and religious lives here in this present world." Evidently, this living good lives is up to us. Even with grace, restraining ourselves and leading good lives is necessary.

So even with the coming of Christ, we are still waiting. For what? "We are waiting in hope for the blessings which will come with the appearance of the glory of our great God and Savior, Christ Jesus."

This is the same Child of Jesus and Mary born in Bethlehem. He was to be called "Emmanuel," that is, *God with us*. He was God with us.

Obviously, Paul is looking here not at the Nativity but at the result of Christ's whole life. What did Christ do? "He sacrificed Himself for us in order to set us free from all wickedness." We see paintings of Mary's Child gazing at a wooden Cross. Mary was warned about something that would pierce her heart.

Christ intended to "purify a people so that they could be His very own and would have no ambitions except to do good."

What is Christmas?

In Luke's Gospel, it says: "Today in the City of David is born to you a Savior who is Christ the Lord" (see Luke 2:11).

Here we see the word *Savior*, the word that Paul later was to use. What is it we are to be saved from? For what? Is it all right if we choose not to know this salvation? Is it all right if our polity seeks to eliminate this good news? Is it all right if we do not teach what happened here?

In a reflection on the long genealogies of Christ's birth in Matthew and Luke, Pope Benedict noted that these lists of ancestors indicate to us that the event of Christ's birth had been long in preparation. What was "new" in Bethlehem had been planned from the foundations of the world. It is intended for "all mankind." *Rejoice and be glad.* "Be not afraid," the shepherds are told. "Grace *is* revealed."

Chapter 7

On the Fear of Christmas[7]

The various enemies of Christmas have managed to remove from public gaze most of the once common external signs of Christmas. We see few mangers. Everything Christian is cleansed and sanitized. "What Christmas is" finds itself removed. One can argue whether things such as the Christmas tree itself, the Yule log, or even snow were not steps to remove any specific Christmas meaning.

Christmas has become a "winter festival," whatever that is. The song "White Christmas" shifted attention from the feast to its atmosphere. "Adeste Fideles" and "Silent Night" we still hear, of course. We try to be "joyful and triumphant," as if the event of Christmas had nothing to do with what causes the joy. We are to be festive without a reason. The increasing emptiness of the feast gnaws at our souls.

Christmas is now a feast without a cause. Folks do not, however, want to give up the days off, the presents, the good feelings, the "chestnuts roasting on an open fire." So they are kept without the religious mood that caused them to come about

---

[7] Published in *The Catholic Thing*, December 2010.

in the first place. We have gone through this elimination-of-Christmas theme before. But what interests me is why Christmas in particular, by all odds the most popular of Christian feasts, has found itself under such attack. We cannot even have symbolic signs of its significance or meaning. Why is Christmas feared? Why is it dangerous?

One reason is, supposedly, that it "offends" those of other religious sensitivities. They have delicate consciences. The older notion of "I will tolerate your quirks if you tolerate mine" is not there. Christmas is what offends. Why is this? Chesterton's poem "The Wise Men" reads:

> Step softly, under snow and rain,
> To find the place where men can pray;
> The way is all so very plain
> That we may lose the way.

Christmas is feared because it is true. If true, it is dangerous. We cannot just ignore it, much as we try.

> So very simple is the road,
> That we may stray from it....
> And the whole Heaven shouts and shakes,
> For God Himself is born again.

We may stray from the road. How odd to have a plain road on which we can lose our way. This not wanting to know about "God Himself" born again is a voluntary act. We do not want to be reminded of the manger. We do not want to see those who rejoice in the Christmas Mass, in the family unity of the Holy Family.

We have instead colors, winter fests, animals, snow, presents. We do not have the manger, the angels singing on high. The

Word made flesh to dwell amongst us? This we do not want to reckon with.

If Christmas is just a myth, we can let it alone. But what if it is a history, an event, an account of what happened in the time of Caesar Augustus, "when the whole world was at peace"? We do everything possible to prevent ourselves from considering the implications of this fact.

The late Christopher Dawson once remarked that, on the morning after the Nativity, the leading papers of Jerusalem, Rome, or Athens did not announce it. It was not important. From the beginning, the Nativity was known by only a few. It was an event that was "too good to be true."

But that is precisely what it is not. It is true. Its good is something we should know and want to know. Indeed, within the Christian corpus is the sometimes upsetting mandate that we are to make this event and its consequences known to "all nations."

Even if they do not want to hear of it?

It seems so.

The fear of Christmas is something even more basic, or perhaps more sinister. Why is that? It is one thing simply not to know something because we have never encountered it or thought about it. It is another thing when, having heard of it, we refuse to allow it to be known. We organize our polity in such a way that every obstacle is put in the way of knowing it.

We are not yet like the countries that seek to prevent private expressions or celebration of Christmas. But, with our increasing denial that marriage is of a man and a woman, we belong to the same mentality. We have taken the first step.

Christmas is a dangerous feast. We fear it. We do not allow ourselves to consider it. Yet, somehow, we still envy those who know this feast of domesticity.

The Reason for the Seasons

"Unto us a Child is born."

"What Child is this?"

If this Child is indeed "Christ the Lord," what happens to us who make every effort to prevent its truth from being known?

Chapter 8

⁀

On Christmas Day[8]

The carol goes: "I saw three ships come sailing in on Christmas Day in the morning." When my brother and his family lived in Aptos, California, after Midnight Mass, after the morning opening of presents, and after breakfast, we would often go down to the nearby beach for a Christmas walk. Many others had the same idea. Children were younger then. You could still say "Merry Christmas" to passersby without fear of violating some unknown federal law.

Down the beach, you could see Santa Cruz with its wharf and boardwalk, while across the water was the outline of the Monterey Peninsula. Whether I ever saw three ships come sailing in to the nearby Capitola Wharf I doubt, but usually smaller craft were on the water in the bright sunshine, so antithetical to the white Christmases of my Iowa boyhood.

Last Christmas I spent with my sister and her family in Chesapeake, Virginia. During the Christmas season, we had an enormous snowfall that blocked most activities for several days. It was, in fact, quite beautiful.

---

[8]   Published in *The Catholic Thing*, December 25, 2012.

The Reason for the Seasons

In addition to mild or snowy days of Christmas stateside, Australian friends tell me that it is midsummer there. One can wonder how cold it was in Bethlehem when Christ was born. I doubt if weather was a factor in the events of this great day; yet it is an element that makes our Christmas days and their memories more vivid.

Of late, I have been struck by the amount of teaching found in the words of the Mass. On Christmas Day, the Missal gives three Prefaces for Christmas. A Preface directs our minds to the fact that Christ, true God and true man, is present at the Consecration.

The second Preface of Christmas begins by addressing the Father. He is all-powerful, ever-living. We place ourselves before Him.

What is our reaction?

The only one it can be. We give thanks. What have we that we have not received? We can only do this "through Christ our Lord." If we did not have Christ, we would never think that giving thanks was ether possible or fitting. Christ gives us title to recognize that the world itself and all of us in it are gifts. We are not products of chance or our own manufacture.

We next tell the Father that He fills us with joy. We see in Him the very love of God. Christmas joy is always special. It is the joy of unexpectedness, of a gift we could never imagine, but one that we would always hope for if we could know it. "No eye can see His glory as our God." We know that hundreds and thousands of people in His time saw the man Christ and did not see Him as God. But He is clearly "one of us."

Who is this Christ born among us this day? We can identify Him. He is the Son of the Father. He was His Son *ante tempora genitus*, "begotten before all ages." That is to say, this Christ first belonged to God. If He is sent to dwell amongst us, He becomes man. But He does not cease to be the Word of the Father within the Trinitarian life of the Godhead.

Thus, He "began in time" (*coepit in tempore*). Time is that thing that we know what it is if we are not asked to define it, as Augustine said. The Gospels are pretty clear on the fact that He began in the time we know. They mention Caesar Augustus, governors of provinces, and Jewish leaders. We are not dealing with myth here. Benedict makes this clear in *Jesus of Nazareth*.

But why did the Father send His Son into the world?

He sent Him to complete something that was intended in the beginning.

What was intended from the beginning?

That all of our kind be able, if they chose, to participate in the inner life of the Trinity.

This is something beyond the powers of our nature. The Fall interfered. The historical record of our need for salvation followed. We needed a redeemer who was to "lift all things to Himself." His coming we call the Incarnation; His birth we call His Nativity. He came to call us back to His "celestial Kingdom."

How are we to respond?

In this event, we are with *omnibus angelis*, all the angels there on the Holy Night. We can only respond with praise, *jucunda celebratione clamantes*; that is, crying out with joyful celebration. We realize that this central event in the divine plan has occurred. The history of the world that goes on into our days remains part of the same plan.

Many do not know of it.

Others refuse to know of it.

But we know and are glad.

Chapter 9

☞

"The Mystery of His Nativity"[9]

The phrase "the mystery of His Nativity" is taken from the Preface of the Masses immediately before Christmas. This wording struck me for several reasons. One has to do with the notion of "mystery." We actually know quite a lot about the Nativity of Christ. We know the place and the circumstances. We know the parents. We know the names of the rulers and emperors at the time.

Much enterprise over the centuries has gone into denying these facts.

Why these denials?

Clearly, it is because these facts are true to careful and responsible investigation; as they are, we cannot maintain that here is just another birth of some unimportant Jewish child during the reign of Caesar Augustus.

Yet, with all the data, we still sense a "mystery." Something more is there.

The more important part of the "mystery" concerning this birth includes the issues of time, place, and circumstances but goes beyond them. "Mystery" does not mean something wholly unknown.

---

[9] Published in *Catholic World Report*, December 21, 2014.

It means, rather, knowing actually and accurately but realizing that more is there to be known. Indeed, in these facts about the time and place of Christ's birth, many may see no "mystery."

Yet, they happened "in the fullness of time," as if to say that they involve a plan, an order, and an intervention. That a child with a name was born of Jewish parents from Nazareth is intelligible. But in Bethlehem when Palestine was under Roman rule, "when the whole world was at peace," is that not provocative?

The birth of any child is something of a "mystery." Why, after all, do any human beings exist in the first place? They do not cause themselves to come to be or to be what they already are. Still, if we look at what is said and handed down about this particular Child, it becomes more complicated, more mysterious. His very name, or one of them, is Emmanuel, which means "God with us." How can God be with us? Why would He want to be? The parents are aware that His origins are more than usual. His disciples come to associate Him with the Word of God. He is "made" flesh. He dwells amongst us. He was from the "beginning," we are told. In Him all things are "made." We hear of the Alpha and the Omega, the beginning and the end. In the "Four Quartets," T. S. Eliot wrote: "In my beginning is my end." How can this be true of all of us unless it be true that the beginning and the end are ordered to each other?

At His birth, Christ's conception becomes public to shepherds, to the world. We wonder about the difference between a child's initial conception and his birth nine months later. A British court decided that a child in the womb was not in law a "person."[10] This

[10] Philippa Taylor, "British Court: Unborn Are 'Organisms,'" Free Republic, December 8, 2014, www.freerepublic.com/focus/f-news/3235022/posts.

arbitrary decision was based on nothing other than the will to allow abortion with legal impunity. Otherwise the whole modern practice of denying the full dignity of a child would be undermined. So the court decided to call what is undoubtedly in the womb before birth simply an "organism." This wording is a form of nominalism. Basically, it is a lie put into law.

But I bring up this recent case for the light that it sheds on the birth of Christ. We know that Herod, when he heard of Christ's birth, sought to kill Him. If Christ really were a king, He would be a threat to Herod's throne. Herod missed killing Christ. His parents quickly bore Him off into Egypt. But Herod did manage instead to kill many other born children under two years old in the area.

It is impossible on any scientific or commonsense grounds to deny the abiding unity of a conceived human person through gestation, to birth, to infancy, adolescence, maturing, old age, and death. If we insist on pretending a discontinuity between conception and birth, we must make the birth of a child, not his conception and gestation, to be a person's "beginning." In modern legal fiction, human birth alone begins personhood. The appearance of any "person" is thus an infinitely more miraculous event than the birth of Christ.

Much British and American law makes the birth of any human person a more mysterious and incoherent event than the birth of God in Christ. If it is the law, not facts, that denies personhood to existing human "organisms," logically the same law for the same reason—namely, whatever the judge or legislator wants—can make an "organism" a "person."

In Christian revelation, the natural order of gestation retains its ordinary integrity. Mary carried and bore a Son.

In the modern legal view, before birth a woman conceives and bears in her womb an "organism," but no "person." The "person" on actual birth is the man from nowhere. If the "organism" is premature, it becomes a "person." The nonpremature "organism" is not a person. The "person" has no real origin. He is a figment of law, not the recognition by the law of a reality that is a human person from his beginning.

We do not claim that Christ came from nowhere. He came from the bosom of the Trinity, where He is the Word. In the fullness of time, He is sent into the world, through the consent of a member of our kind, His mother, Mary. He is true God and true man.

The "mystery" of Christ's Nativity thus lands us right in the midst of our present-day reality. We see what are supposed to be "learned" judges forced to deny reality so that eliminating human persons before their birth can be "legal." No judge seems to be brave enough to say that a child in the womb is what all of us, including the judge himself, once were and now are, namely, human persons. It would be more tolerable and more intellectually honest to say simply, with Herod, that it is legal to kill any person under two years old. Not a few philosophers do propose this position. They merely move the law to two years after birth before "personhood" is established. In a contorted way, this lethal method seems better than to lie and to pretend that the same "organism" suddenly and mysteriously, immediately after its birth, becomes a "person."

"The light shines in the darkness and the darkness comprehendeth it not" (John 1:5). The only addendum that needs to be made to these considerations on the Nativity of Christ is that the word "person" itself, a word from Greek drama, came to be the very word used to indicate the uniqueness of Father, Son, and Spirit within the Godhead. Each Person is itself fully God, fully open to the other Persons but not becoming them.

"The Mystery of His Nativity"

When the Word, the Second Person, became man, He taught us that all persons, from their real beginnings in eternity, in their conception and in their nativity, are open, if they would receive it, to the life that the Son offers in a gift to all in His birth. The British and other courts seem shrouded in a darkness that refuses to see the light shining on what is right before them.

"No one has ever seen God. It is God, the only Son, ever at the Father's side, who has revealed Him" (John 1:18). This is the "mystery" that Christ's Nativity announces.

Chapter 10

⤜

"A Raging Mirth"[11]

A student gave me G. K. Chesterton's *Poems*, a handsome book. In it are love, war, religious, and miscellaneous poems, ballads, and "Rhymes for the Times." Its most famous poem is probably "Lepanto." Its most intriguing is "Antichrist; or The Reunion of Christendom, an Ode."

The religious poems are often about Christmas, a favorite theme of Chesterton. For my own Christmas reflection, I single out "A Child of the Snows." Such a title gives me pause when I think of my friends in Australia, for whom Christmas is not snowy, nor is it for my California family. But wintry Christmas scenes are common for many.

The poem begins with the statement that we hear a "hymn" that will never be "heard again." The nights are very dark. Yet this "dark is alive with rain." With rain, the night is not dead. Rain causes life. Living in "sleet and snow" makes us aware of "where the great fires are."

This is not Hell, with its own brand of fires, that we are looking at.

---

[11] Published in *Inside Catholic*, December 25, 2010.

The Reason for the Seasons

At the center of the earth, we find fire and heat, but here on the surface we do not find fire but rather "a raging mirth." This line is mindful of the end of *Orthodoxy*. There, we discovered that the one thing that Christ held back from us was His "mirth." He held it back, not because He did not have it, but because, for now, we could not bear it.

On such a night we recall the "Ancient Inn," where the Child is found. We follow the feet "where all souls meet." Fra Angelico's painting in the National Gallery shows streams and streams of people processing to the crib, the Inn, where Mary, Joseph, and the Child are found.

Where or what exactly is this? It is the "Inn at the End of the World."

Here is another powerful Chestertonian image. The Inn at the End of the World was in a short essay by Chesterton about a town in France. And, of course, it is in the last lines of *Dickens*, where we shall meet in serious joy as we drink from the great flagons at this Inn at the End of the World. I have always loved that Inn, I must confess. I do think that it is where our steps are taking us.

But this is the first time that I have seen it identified with the "Ancient Inn" where the Child was born. Where else could it be?

Reminiscent of Nietzsche, we are next reminded that the "gods lie dead." Mass readings during the last days of the Liturgical Year often refer to the end of the world. The sun will be darkened. Here "the flame of the sun is flown." The classical gods lie "cold." All their good, as Chesterton said, is saved in Christianity. The ancient world's sanity is found in the worship of those who walk in procession. They saved what could be saved. Christmas transforms their Winter Feast.

Where these "gods lie dead," what do we find?

"A Raging Mirth"

"A Child comes forth alone." He does not come from the pagan gods. He is an "only-begotten Son." His origin is not ultimately from mortal men, though He becomes flesh and dwells amongst us, "born of the Virgin, Mary."

"A raging mirth" is found at the center of the world. That mirth is the real fire found there. The Inn at the End of the World is located at the "Ancient Inn." There the Child came forth "alone." But He was not alone. He was from the Father. He was Logos, Word. We are all made in His image and likeness.

Christmas, Chesterton insisted, is the Feast of the Home, our Home. On Christmas Eve, we should lock our doors and be with our family, with those we love and who love us. The Child who came forth "alone" always spoke of His father as "My Father." He told us to address Him as "Our Father." But if the gods are dead, the Father is alive. He gives life and light that was to shine in a darkness, which comprehended it not.

The dark is alive with rain. The hymn of the angels will "never be heard again." Glory to God in the highest.

On earth, we are not yet at the highest. Yet we are to drink from the great flagons at the Inn at the End of the World, with its "raging mirth." Once we know of the Child who is alone and of His sacrifice, we are no longer called servants but friends. That is what this "Ancient Inn" brought about. Those in the "Inn at the End of the World" stretch out to receive the "raging mirth." This, too, is what Christmas is about.

Chapter 11

⌒

"Only Where She Was Homeless"[12]

Chesterton's poem "The House of Christmas" is found in Kevin Belmont's *A Year with G. K. Chesterton*. I had never seen this poem before, though many of its themes are familiar to lovers of Chesterton.

The central institution of the family, whose integrity this feast divinely reaffirms, has never been under more direct attack than in today's political order. What the Devil hates most, it is said, is the innocent human child. He shows it by having men and women kill their own, with the active collaboration of their states.

Indeed, an old tradition maintains that the fall of the angels occurred when they were given a vision of the Incarnation, the Word as a human child, at which some rebelled. Such a creature was far beneath the angels in their order of being. It was an insult to the angels that the Word was made flesh.

The state increasingly takes over the functions of the human family. It puts children in schools and day-care centers as soon

---

[12] Published in *Gilbert Magazine*, December 2013.

as possible after birth. It tells mothers they are free to do what they want. The state will provide.

More and more, we see the very begetting of children in arrangements outside the monogamous family and contrary to its nature and spirit. As a result, we become, all of us, homeless, with no hope of finding or founding a home. In a civil society without real homes, no one can be "homesick," for no one has a home. No one is connected with that Home to which all the real hopes of mankind inevitably point, through the love and intimacy that are first learned in a home.

Chesterton's is a poem about the Nativity, of the home that is no home.

> In the place where she [Mary] is homeless
> All men are at home.

The notion of home and homelessness is found everywhere in Chesterton. Christ is not born in the home of Joseph and Mary in Nazareth, but in an Inn that became the place in which we can best see what a Holy Family really is.

The existential experience that human beings have, or ought to have, is that of "being homesick at home." It is a paradox, this spending our lives longing to return home, only, on gaining it, to find ourselves yet homesick. "For men are homesick in their homes."

"'Homesick' for what?" we might wonder.

It is for the place where "all men are at home."

Chesterton has often made it clear that, on Christmas Eve, we should shut our doors and be with our family, with those we love and to whom we are committed. In this world, we do not want all men to be in one home or in one state, but each in his own home. We want many states, not one. The experience of each home cannot be replicated. We wish that each man and woman have together their own home, with their own offspring.

Why is it that home is so intimately associated with Christmas? Do not pagans have homes? In the English-speaking world, no doubt, it has something to do with Dickens, with Scrooge, Tiny Tim, and Christmas at the Cratchits. But they did not "invent" Christmas. Rather they celebrated it as something handed down to them.

> Only where He was homeless
> Are you and I at home.

This sentence is very poignant. Only if He suffers can you and I be forgiven. Joseph, Mary, and Jesus did not, after all, stay in the Inn. They went back to their home in Nazareth, only soon to leave for Egypt and then to return again. Homelessness cannot be the permanent condition of mankind.

> To an open house in the evening
> Home shall men come,
> To an older place than Eden
> And a taller town than Rome.

What place, we might ask, is "older" than Eden?

What town is taller than Rome?

Implicitly, here, Chesterton recalls our theology. The Incarnation was not itself the beginning. Rome, the great city, was not the Eternal City. The world was conceived within the bosom of the Trinity. The City of God is the community of the Father, the Son, and the Spirit.

If we put these truths together, we realize that Eden was itself the result of the divine plan to create a world in which beings, who were not themselves gods, could live and decide. Eden was the place of their decision to accept God's city or their own. The Incarnation was God's response to man's choice not to accept what he was intended to be and to be given. The ultimate origin of man is not man. "Before Abraham was, I am" (see John 8:58). "I knew you before you were in your mother's womb" (see Jer. 1:5). This is why we are homesick at home, but we are intended to have homes.

"To the things that cannot be and that are," Chesterton continues. He is paradoxical here. Obviously, things that are can come to be, as they evidently did. Yet these things, this creation, this Incarnation, these are beyond our imagination that they could be. The things that cannot be, are. We behold them and are glad.

> To the place where God was homeless
> And all men are at home.

The place where God was homeless was in the Inn. But because He came to be, we all can return to that place, that City of God, that inner life of the Trinity, in which and for which we were originally intended to be. All men are only at home if they choose to pass through the place where Christ was homeless. He entered this world and left it where His mother was present, at the crib and at the Cross, as if to tell us what to be prepared for in our homes of men whence we return on our way to the eternal life for which we are born, even in this world.

Chapter 12

⌒

The Essence of Christmas[13]

In an old *Peanuts* cartoon, Lucy approaches Charlie Brown with a large piece of paper in hand. She tells him: "This is my 'git' list, Charlie Brown." While Charlie looks on in amazement, Lucy explains: "These are all the things I figure I'm gonna 'git' for Christmas from my two grandpas and two grandmas, and eight uncles and aunts!"

Logically, Charlie inquires: "Where is your 'give' list?"

Lucy, taken aback, replies: "My what?"

While Lucy looks on uncomprehendingly, Charlie walks away in disgust saying, "I knew it!"

This sequence, of course, fits in perfectly with the self-centered character of the delightful Lucy. Her thing is "gitting," not giving. We have all heard St. Paul's statement "It is more blessed to give than to receive" (Acts 20:35). Not necessarily excluding ourselves, we encounter friends or relatives who are primarily takers, not givers. Aristotle said somewhere that everybody loves those who are generous with their wealth, the "givers," in other words.

---

[13] Published in *The Hoya*, December 2012.

The Reason for the Seasons

The primary analogate for Christmas is the birth of Christ. We see the eventual arrival of the Wise Men, who bring gifts of "gold, frankincense, and myrrh." Behind the scenes is Christ Himself, the very understanding of whom requires a reflection on giftedness, on something offered not in justice, but in generosity.

Some people think that everything that I "give" to someone else is something taken away from me. Such is a "zero-sum" view of the world: there is only so much; nothing can be replaced. With such a presupposition, everything and everybody are on edge. Generosity is almost impossible. Everyone is at war with everyone else about "his own."

The world, however, is not created in parsimoniousness. Its origin is in gift and abundance. Real wealth in the world is not in some deposit of things, be it oil or coal or gold or whatever. The ultimate wealth in the world is found in the human mind as it thinks about what is out there, not of its own making.

When we think of giving, we must start with loving. Properly speaking, to love means to wish not one's own good but the good of the person who is loved. We always find a certain selflessness about it. It is true that we long for reciprocity, but that too is a gift that we cannot demand.

If we look at St. Paul's famous dictum about its being better to give than to receive, we can surely understand the point that giving seems more selfless than receiving. Yet, thanks to a professor I once had here at Georgetown, I have often thought that in many ways receiving is more indicative of our character than giving.

As we approach Christmas, as we recall our childhood memories of Christmas, we have little difficulty in understanding Lucy's "git" list. Christmas was a time in which we were given things. We anticipated it. What seemed so extraordinary about

Christmas was the unnecessity of it all. Christmas was not really the time to be given something we needed but precisely something that we did not need or expect. We found something abundant about it, something almost playful, intended not for need but for delight.

A proud man may give gifts, but it takes a rather humble man to receive them. In this sense, the ability graciously to receive gifts is much more revealing of our souls than our giving things. The man to whom nothing can be given, it strikes me, is isolated. I do not mean here that a rich man may not need anything. Quite the opposite. A gift is really, at bottom, not constituted primarily by what is given but by its symbol or meaning. The gift stands in the giver's stead.

The fact that the birth of Christ is primarily associated with an unexpected gift, the Child Himself, reminds us of the fact that children are not the products of economic or scientific enterprises. They are gifts. Parents do not somehow manufacture their children. Children come as an overflow of a mutual love, not as a planned production.

Parents meet their children for the first time when they are born. Their children are given. To be parents, parents must be receivers of gifts, in this case of the most precious of all gifts given to mankind.

So what do we "git" for Christmas?

Not just "presents," but indications that we are loved. We read in Scripture that "God so loved the world that He gave His only-begotten Son" (John 3:16). This is why, I think, the great mystery of Christmas lies not so much in the fact that we are given much, but in the way we receive it. We do not have control over what we are given. We reveal our souls in how we receive it.

Chapter 13

⤳

Christmas 2011[14]

A student of mine gave me a book for the end of a semester. She is Jewish but wanted to give me a Christmas card with it. She told me, "I looked, but there are no 'Christmas cards' in the shop, only 'holiday cards.'" Her card said, "Seasons Greetings." It was decorated with shiny green leaves and an elegant red artificial flower. One has to be touched by the effort.

This comment about "holiday cards" made me take a second look at the cards I have already received. I tend to get actual Christmas cards. From Australia, I have a card with a green wreath on a door with "An Irish Christmas Blessing for You and Yours." The blessing reads: "May your hearth be ever warm, your table ever full, your joys ever new, your love ever growing, and your memories everlasting," followed by something that is probably "Merry Christmas" in Gaelic.

The Christmas card of the president of Georgetown shows a lovely sketch of our elegant gothic Healy Building from below the library steps. Off the steps, a lamp post with a green wreath and a red bow are seen.

---

[14] Published in *Ignatius Insight*, December 23, 2011.

The Reason for the Seasons

Friends in Salinas, California, who visited me this year in Georgetown, sent a lovely Madonna and Child card with the words "Peace on Earth."

Another friend in Virginia sent a very cute card with three identical little angels, each with hands folded, blond hair, and halo. Two have eyes piously closed, but the last one has hers wide open, and we see her toes sticking out of from under her long gown.

Many cards have photos of some family scene, often before a Christmas tree, snow, or festive background. This sort of card keeps visual touch with growing and changing families.

From England, I have a card, a sketch on red paper showing a happy Joseph and Mary gazing at the Child in a crib with the star behind and above them.

From my Catholic Indian friends, Maya and Peeya, I have a card with "Christ Is Born." Against a night scene, we see a hut, a stable with Joseph and Mary. Light shines on the Child. Behind we see a faint Crucifixion against the back wall. On the sides, a sheep and a donkey gaze into the scene.

From friends in Aptos, California, I have a very lovely scene with Mary sleeping and a very handsome Joseph holding the baby; again, we are in a grotto while a donkey and a sheep look on from behind.

From the widow of one of my cousins in Iowa, I have a card showing Joseph with a staff, leading a donkey on which Mary is sitting sidesaddle. The star is behind them; they are still going to Bethlehem.

From Florida, I have a different version of the same scene, a much more tropical setting against a palm tree.

From England again, I have a lovely card of a stone Irish Cross sitting alone in a wintry scene, against a stone fence and gate.

Reddish hills are seen in the background. The script is "Peace of the Season."

From Missouri, I have a card that shows a crowded scene in the Inn-stable. The donkey is right on top of the crib looking in. The sheep is on the other side. The shepherds are there along with what looks like the three kings. Another donkey and sheep are at the side.

The card from my cousin in Detroit shows a very lovely winter scene, with snow falling on the pines. "A Christmas Wish: May God's peace surround you this Christmas and always." That is quite nice.

Finally, from Kentucky, we see a small church in the woods. We see a brook with a stone bridge over it. A horse pulls a man in a small sleigh toward the church. Snow is falling all around; heavy snow is already on the ground. Lights come through the church windows.

Christmas is not what we call a "holiday."

Christmas is a "holy" day, which is what the word *holiday* really means.

It is not a good idea to pass through the Christmas season without reflecting on what it is. Catholicism is an intellectual religion. The feast of Christmas follows logically from the Annunciation, from the Incarnation. It points to the adolescence, to the public life of Christ; then as several cards depicted, to His Crucifixion. It is the same man who is "conceived by the Holy Spirit," who is "born" in Nazareth, during the reign of Caesar Augustus.

It is my view that the reason we no longer see many "Christmas cards" has to do with a deliberate choice, a conscious choice that we "will" not know, that we "will" not allow anyone to think of what the Nativity of Christ might entail.

Christmas Cards do not disappear for no reason.

The Reason for the Seasons

In one sense, we can say that they disappear because there is no "demand." It is a market thing. There is some truth to this. Today, if we buy a nice card and mail it, the cost is not insignificant. We can now e-mail our greetings to Aunt Margaret for nothing; we can even tune in to her living room and chat.

Christmas is a public feast that, at its best, is wholly private. No one really knew the significance of the event in Bethlehem at the time it happened. God did not come into the world in power and drama. A few shepherds noticed, but even they had to be prodded by sounds and sights, by curiosity.

Soon the couple known as Joseph and Mary packed up and went home with the new baby who was not, evidently, born where He was by total accident, even if it looked as if He were. No sooner had they got there than they had to pack up again and be off to Egypt. It seems that the king saw this Child as his potential rival. He even killed young boys who might be this man that the Magi evidently told him about.

What is the Nativity?

The Lord now actually appears.

He is no longer in eternity, no longer in the womb of Mary.

He is already a sign of contradiction. Many of the prophets of Israel longed to see what those shepherds saw and did not see it. Why did they not see? Was it because they were blind? They had eyes. But they did not want to see. They had to lie to themselves lest they see.

What exactly happened here?

The Child who was born was Christ the Lord. To explain Him, we need to talk accurately, to distinguish. If we get it wrong, we won't know. If we get it right, we will see a plan being worked out in the person, in the life and death of this Child now born in Bethlehem.

Christmas cards, in fact, often do a good job at depicting what actually happened there in the stable, with the donkey and sheep, with the shepherds and Joseph and Mary.

Great things do not always happen in great ways, or at least, in ways we think are great. But great things did happen here, once, and once only. It was not necessary for Christ to come more than once into this world, our world. His reality is still present. We seek to flee its import to us. We want every explanation but the one that explains.

Christmas is about the Word becoming flesh and dwelling amongst us. The Word is within the Godhead, in His active, eternal life. The Word seeks to lead us back to the purpose for which we are created, to share His eternal life. These things really happened. The world cannot pretend that they did not happen, though it has no alternative if it does not want to know the truth of who He was.

Christmas 2011 is in its very name: the "Mass" of Christmas, the Nativity of the Lord among us, the Word made flesh, the dwelling amongst us. These things we know and ponder.

The song goes, "Joy to the world." Not joy for no reason. Joy because the Lord has come. We did not know He was coming. He came to dwell amongst us that we might eternally dwell with Him. There is no other reason, no other explanation of our being, of "why we are rather than are not."

We are now at an advanced stage of our civilization wherein we have to say to our friends: "Pardon me, would you mind if I wished you a Merry Christmas?" The only people who mind, I suspect, are those who are worried that what the Christians say about who is born in Bethlehem might be true.

They prefer not to know.

And that defines their souls.

Chapter 14

⌒

The Nativity[15]

The Word was made flesh, and dwelt among us.

—John 1:14, KJV

We begin with the Beginning. The Word was with God. The Word was God. Flesh did not make the Word. What "dwelt among us" was the Word, the Logos, nothing less. This is a fact. The whole world is different because of it. The whole world exists, though it need not have existed. And if it "need not," why does it exist?

The Spirit of God is called the Gift: Father, Son, Spirit, one God. The English poet Robert Southwell, in his "Nativity of Christ," writes:

> Gift better than himself God doth not know;
> Gift better than his God no man can see.
> This gift doth here the giver given bestow;
> Gift to this gift let each receiver be.
> God is my gift, Himself He freely gave me;
> God's gift am I, and none but God shall have me.

[15] Published in *Inside Catholic*, December 25, 2007.

The Reason for the Seasons

The world is the gift of the Giver to those who can freely receive it. Not only is the whole of the cosmos God's gift, but it would not have been given unless someone within it could say, "God's gift am I." We are made in the image of God. "Gift to this gift let each receiver be." We are first "receivers," having been received. This is our glory.

The Incarnation means that the Second Person of the Trinity, called "Word" within the Godhead, became man. *Homo factus est.* Once we are born, we dwell amidst our kind. This event, this Birth, of which we speak happened once during the reign of Caesar Augustus, "when the world was at peace."

The Nativity of the Logos was not a myth, nor an imagination. The world is no longer the same because of it. Because of it, the world can be what it was intended to be from the beginning. How could the world be, granted that *ex nihilo, nihil fit?* If the Word of the Godhead is born amongst us, something is being said to us about what we are, why we are. The Word addresses hearers of words. All things are changed. Man can know what he is only when he knows what this Incarnation was.

We begin in conception. *The Angel of the Lord said unto Mary.* We proceed to birth, to the Nativity. *Glory to the newborn King.* The Nativity means that what is inside the mother now appears in the visible world. *Mary pondered these things in her heart.* We begin our celebration of new life with its nativity, when we can see and touch it. We rightly remember the day of our birth, not that of our conception, which is much more obscure, however much it is our real origin in this world. We count our years from the date of our own nativity.

The birth of a child takes place in a given time and place. At least the mother is present, and hopefully the father and other relatives and friends. Even though human birth is in pain, when the new life is once present, there, visibly, joy appears to those who behold it. The father is now present. He begins to see. Things have to be done. He must do them.

At Christ's birth, in Bethlehem, the words "We bring you tidings of great joy" are heard (see Luke 2:10). Not just joy, but "great" joy.

The aged Simeon said, "This child is destined for the fall and rise of many in Israel" (Luke 2:34).

The faithful—all of them—are invited to come, even to come "joyful and triumphant." Why are they to be "joyful and triumphant?" One cannot be "joyful and triumphant" unless he has a reason. Do we have a reason?

"God is my gift, Himself He freely gives me."

The Nativity of Christ did occur. We are not idealists. We are able to affirm *what is*, that it is. The paradox: the gift of God is Himself, freely given to me in His Incarnation and Nativity. Even when I am first a gift, a further gift is given to me: "grace upon grace." The receiver of gifts is himself a gift. This is our metaphysics, grace upon grace.

The kind of being we are, from the beginning, from every nativity, is intended to see God face-to-face. We can reject this gift, this gift upon gift. We are given an end beyond our nature. We are fallen and redeemed.

Christmas is the feast of the Nativity, of the Word now made flesh and visible to us. When the Word is made flesh, nothing is the same. Now we can return, if we will, to that for which we are created. God created the world so that within the world would be those to whom He could give His inner life. There is only one temptation: to make our end less than it was intended for us to know. "Behold I bring you tidings of great joy, for today is born to us a Son who is Christ the Lord" (see Luke 2:10–11).

Chapter 15

The "Word Became Man among Men"[16]

There is one God, who by His word and wisdom created all things and set them in order. His Word is our Lord Jesus Christ, who in this last age became man among men to unite end and beginning, that is, man and God.

—St. Irenaeus, *Against Heresies* 4:20

Catholicism concerns itself with understanding. We do not believe just because we believe. We believe on the basis of evidence, of argument, or of authority. We want to grasp the basis of what we know. We know that many arguments are illogical or unconvincing. We also hold some things that are considered to be true because other people witnessed an event and understood an argument.

Most of the things we take for granted every day are held because of the authority of someone else. If we want to know if our milk is safe to drink or our meat suitable to eat, we take the testimony of the inspectors, merchants, and farmers. Unless we have serious doubts about the quality of this particular bottle of

[16] Published in Aleteia.org, December 24, 2013.

milk or slice of meat, we go ahead unconcerned to drink or eat it. We don't get sick. The authority was trustworthy. Authority itself, however, is always based on someone actually seeing the event or knowing the argument. Authority does not exist for authority's sake.

Revelation also contains truths that describe reality. Some of these are more essential than others, but all relate to the central fact of our existence and how it came about. "How can we talk about God today?" Benedict XVII asked.

> The first answer is that we can talk about God because he has talked to us; so the first condition for speaking of God is listening to what God himself has said.... God is therefore not a distant hypothesis concerning the world's origin; he is not a mathematical intelligence who is far from us.[17]

God wants us to know Him, ourselves, and the world, as we learn in Scripture.

But does not Scripture send us confusing messages?

After all, many versions of Christianity exist, not all compatible with each other. We should not be overly surprised by the confusion that exists because of disunity among Christians about what it is they hold. We often "listen" to what God has to tell us, but we only "hear" what we want to put into our own lives.

The Church exists precisely to deal with this issue. She exists to make sure that what is basic — what is originally taught — remains the same, remains what is handed down.

Aquinas tells us that the Word of God is our first teacher. We do not improve on its essence. Rather, in our humanity, we are, if

[17] Audience, November 28, 2012.

we seek to understand and practice revelation, made more what we are. That is, when we deal with God's revelation, we are not seeking to find something better than what God has revealed to us about what we are. When we "hear" what God wants us to be, we know that this is what is best for us.

We ourselves do not know fully what we are intended to be. We can figure out a few things. We are pretty sure we are meant to be happy, even when we are, in fact, not very happy. But this is still vague. We need to have it "fleshed out" more clearly. And in fact, it was quite literally "fleshed out" as we discover in revelation. "The Word was made 'flesh.'"

As Irenaeus intimates, this word *flesh* means "man," human being. We were intended to be what we are: not gods, not rabbits, but men, beings with minds that unsettle us when we do not understand something. We are especially unsettled when we do not understand ourselves. We cannot understand ourselves solely by ourselves. This is because that for which we exist is more than is due to us. We exist supernaturally, not just naturally.

What does this odd way of speaking mean?

As Irenaeus said, in us the end will be united in the beginning. What does this mean?

All things are "set in order," as Irenaeus put it. From the beginning we are created to live a life that is more than we can expect. We are to share in the inner life of the Godhead. This destiny would seem unlikely were it not for Christ's being sent into the world. Word was made flesh. He who is God became, while remaining God, also man. When we understand this connection, we see, through the testimony of others, that knowing God is possible. Indeed, it is what the world is about. The Incarnation and Nativity are to be understood. God now has a voice to which we listen.

Chapter 16

⌒

The Nativity: What Is It?[18]

A Filipina lady whom I know told me that her mother was born on Christmas Day—*La Natividad.* So, naturally, her parents named her Natividad or, shortened, Navidad. Jose Feliciano's now famous Christmas song, "Feliz Navidad," remains one of the most popular and widely enjoyed of modern Christmas songs. "Happy Nativity"—"Merry Christmas"—"Feliz Navidad." At Christmas, my sister plays this song on her piano.

The Mormon church in Palo Alto has an annual display of crèches from around the world. Evidently, the Mormon world-wide mission endeavor resulted in many missionaries bringing home artifacts from various places around the globe. In the general Palo Alto area, moreover, many people have crèches they have collected over the years. In total, there seem to be some fifteen hundred elaborate, multifigured scenes of the Nativity, from Mexico, Peru, Cambodia, Africa, Germany, Switzerland, American Indian tribes, Portugal, and just about anywhere. There was a lovely dark-blue Murano glass Madonna. Each year some 350 of these different Nativity scenes are displayed in a

---

[18] Published in Aleteia.org, December 24, 2014.

lovely setting in the church halls. Striking figures of Joseph, Mary, and the Child, the Wise Men, the shepherds, the animals of all sorts, and even carved breads and eggs are displayed. The dress of Mary and Joseph, as well as their facial features, usually reflect the time and country of origin of the artist.

The Nativity—what is it?

It comes from the Latin, "to be born."

What is the origin of any child born into this world?

We really must recall that any born child is already a conceived child, with a nine-month inner-worldly record already in place. At the moment of his conception, all that he is, his unique being, is already present. What is left for this child is simply to grow, to become fully what he already is, a human being, male or female. No parents know ahead of time just what this child begotten of them is like. Although ultrasounds can follow his development, they have to wait to find out by seeing the child once born. Then they see him grow, develop into what he already is. The birth of a child is, at the same time, both an astonishment and a lesson in the responsible care of another, as if to say that the latter, the care, flows from the former, the amazement, that such a new thing could exist as it is at all.

Yet no child is understood if he is considered to originate in absolutely nothing, if he is held to be a total product of chance. His very body is related to the genes and looks that belonged to his grandparents and ancestors on both sides of his family. His soul—that which makes him human as such—originates in God. It is, though related to a body, itself immaterial, hence immortal.

Human life, moreover, has origins in the Godhead. Before we were in our mother's womb, God knew us. But He did not know us apart from our parents or them apart from their parents. We are always individual persons yet related to others, and they to us. This interchange constitutes our lives.

Such reflections have two implications.

Our very being is ultimately found within God's intention to create the world in the first place. In doing so, each of us is included. We do not have any choice about whether we will be given existence. If we did have such a choice, it would logically mean that we existed as we are before we existed as we are at birth.

Our parents do not engineer us. All they know is that children can be born of them. They never know which ones until they see them. Our conception and birth, in other words, are best understood as a gift, not as something "due" or constructed. Yet, once we are conceived, our growth, which needs love, help, and attention, proceeds by the necessity of our being what we are. We will reach infancy, youth, middle age, old age, and death. The only way to stop this subsequent flourish as a human being is to kill it, though such a killing does not prevent that which is killed from reaching the purpose for which it was made in the Godhead.

The second consequence of our having an origin in the Godhead is that while we are related to others of our kind—we are familial, social, and political beings—we are also present to God, who sustains our being in its very existence. Something inexhaustible is discovered in each human being, reflecting back on himself. As we proceed to know one another, we always find some inexhaustible depth in ourselves and in our neighbor, something that we did not put there, something we cannot fully fathom. Our being reaches unto the Godhead, in which the idea of our existence first resided.

The Reason for the Seasons

St. Augustine, in his *Confessions*, guides us to the understanding that God is not only in the world but also within us, sustaining us, loving us. This divine presence is the source of our dignity, of the fact that even God treats us after the manner of His creation, after the manner of what we are. This truth is why our relation to God is both indirect, through the *things that are*, and direct, through our reflecting on the divine presence sustaining us in being, in loving us.

* * *

We can, of course, refuse to be what we are.

This refusal explains, in part, why we have the Nativity of the Child of the Holy Family. "Nativity" here means not just the birth of any given person, but the birth of the Son of God into this world at a definite time and in a definite place, when Caesar Augustus was Roman emperor. Early Christian heresies are largely complicated efforts *not* to admit that Christ, the Child born in Bethlehem, was both true man, hence born of woman, and true God, hence the Son of the Father within the Godhead, the Logos, the eternally begotten Word, who fully knows the Father.

But this Christ was born in the City of David. He is Christ the Lord. This Nativity of the Son into the world is sometimes called by Church Fathers His "second" birth, since He was first born, begotten not made, of or from the Father within the Trinity before all ages, a phrase that does not imply a time when the Word was not.

As with all births, Christ's birth was also a looking forward. Simeon warned Mary that a sword would pierce her heart. And it did. The Nativity of Christ begins a relatively short life of only thirty-three years, much of which was "hidden," as they say.

The Nativity: What Is It?

Looking back on Christ's life, the evangelists began to consider what they knew of Christ's birth and the town in which He lived. Subsequent generations recalled what they knew of Christ's birth in the light of His subsequent life. They often tried to reproduce or narrate its setting. Simeon, on seeing this Child in the Temple with His parents, tells us that "my eyes have seen the salvation of Israel" (see Luke 2:30). Imagine saying this! "My" eyes have *seen*, not thought about, the "salvation" while he was looking at an Infant.

"Salvation" first had to do with a person, then, on His maturity, on His explaining what it is He knew of His Father, of His plan for our salvation. The Nativity of Christ is not an abstraction; it is not just a nice idea. It is a real birth. And who is this Child? Why bother about Him? If He were just another child born into the Roman Empire, we would not need to pay so much attention to Him. But if He is indeed the Word, the Son of the Father, made man, the whole world is changed. But we can find reasons not to accept this fact. We can find reasons to deny that it is a fact. What we cannot do is change the fact. The Christian calendar calls each year after this birth *in Anno Domini* — in the year of the Lord.

Has the full reason Christ became men been completed? Evidently not. Why not? No doubt, it has much to do with "the day and the hour known only to the Father," with the purpose of this Incarnation, with the constant re-presentation to mankind in the Nativity that, yes, this was the Son of God sent into your world. There will not be another. All needed evidence has already been presented. Each year this Nativity is celebrated again. Its story, its songs, its lore are known to us. We notice an increasing rejection of it, a wanting not even to hear about it.

The Reason for the Seasons

"Why is this?" we wonder.

In spite of the evidence, many *want* it not to be true. They build their lives and their polities on this premise. Two kinds of "silent night" exist. One is rooted in awe and glory; the other in the rejection of the two gifts, the two nativities that constitute our being and our salvation.

Chapter 17

Christmas: The Reason for the Season[19]

Since Christmas in the northern part of the Northern Hemisphere occurs just after the winter solstice, it is difficult for us to imagine a Christmas in Australia or Chile, where the weather is summery, not wintry. Actually, Christmas in California, where I live, is closer to summer climates than to the winter ones of the higher mountains or of the weather farther north. Many of the sentimental Christmas songs recall winter scenes or moods. I believe there are Aussie versions of many songs such as "Jingle Bells." Actually, the average temperature in Bethlehem on Christmas is about that of Lake City, Florida, about 43 degrees — chilly, but not the Canadian Rockies. When my brother lived in Santa Cruz, California, we often took a long walk on a warm beach on Christmas Day.

We do not really know the actual date of Christ's birth. The Gospels only indicate that He was born, and where and under what circumstances (both locally in a manger and internationally under the decree of Caesar Augustus that the whole world should be enrolled). December 25 is celebrated exactly nine months

[19] Published in MercatorNet, December 18, 2014.

after the feast of Christ's Annunciation to Mary, on March 25. But the date in December probably had something to do with Christianizing the Roman celebrations of winter.

Does it matter that Christ was not born in the Outback of Australia or the southern island of New Zealand or near Beijing or Calcutta? In one sense, we can probably say no. But that no would require a whole other narrative of divine intervention into this world whereby this event would be explicable. Indeed, none of these countries would be today the way it is, if the Nativity of Christ had not taken place where and when it did.

If anything is clear, it is that the Incarnation and birth of Christ involved Jewish, not Chinese, Hindu, or other backgrounds. The relation of Christianity to Greece and Rome is, of course, also intimately bound up with these events in the Palestine of Christ's birth. Both Alexander the Great and the Romans had the idea of world empire, of one language, one law, and one brotherhood. Christianity, when it sorted itself out, found room for the Jewish, Roman, and Greek traditions within its overall coherent understanding of reality. It is with this background that it initially faced the world.

Christmas is the feast of the home.

At its best, it needs children, older and younger, grandparents, aunts, uncles, and cousins. We live in a world dangerously close to eliminating co-lateral lines of family. Much of the growing secular intolerance of Christmas is a rejection of human life as such. Yet when Christianity is in trouble, the home is in trouble. Chesterton, whose Christmas memories are full of Dickens's Christmases, remarked that, at Christmas, we should finally shut the doors of our home and be there with our family.

Christ was not actually born in the home of Joseph and Mary, but in the town of David, not even in the Inn, a good distance from Nazareth. He is thus known as Jesus of Nazareth, not Jesus of Bethlehem. He was a small-town boy. In the town of His birth today and in the areas surrounding it, we find fewer and fewer Christians. Muslim discrimination and threats are evident to them. So they migrate to the Americas or wherever they can enter. Plus, they too, like Catholics in Italy and Spain, have very low birth rates. They are aware that the Jihadists and their sympathizers strive to eliminate all Christians from Muslim lands, lands that were once mostly Christian.

Something providential is probably going on here, though one would be loath to speculate on what it is.

In general, the Jews, the Muslims, the Buddhists, the Chinese, and the Hindus have been impervious to the impact of Christ's birth.

At various periods in postbiblical history, significant efforts have been made to convert China, India, Japan, and the Muslim lands. There are said to be many covert Christians in China today, but the only "Catholic" country in the Far East is the Philippines.

Australia and New Zealand certainly have a strong Christian presence, as do Korea and Vietnam. These lands have learned modern technology and economic methods without significantly changing their belief structure. Why did not Muslim lands, China, India, Africa, or some other lands first develop what we know as science today? Not a few hold that the reason is theological, but there is no doubt that ideologies from communism to philosophical religions like Hinduism can absorb the technical side of modern science.

* * *

From the human side, Christmas, literally the "Mass of Christ," was not first an idea. It was first an event, even though an event with origins in the Godhead itself. The Christmas Mass is the memorial each year of this event. Or, perhaps better, the Mass is the memorial of Christ's Passion, death, and Resurrection, the sacrifice, in other words, of the Child who was conceived of the Holy Spirit and born in Bethlehem.

The event of Christ has been often seen as only the birth of another man. Almost every conceivable effort has been made to show either (1) that Christ never existed or (2) that He was not God. It is instructive to recognize that atheism, disbelief in God, is far less prevalent and significant than the denial both of the humanity and divinity of Christ. Belief or proof of God's existence is not nearly so much doubted as the coming of God into the world as also man.

The reasons for this difference are instructive. No doubt, an atheist is not likely to affirm the divinity of a Christ. He is not really much concerned about Christ except indirectly insofar as He is said to be God. But historically, even many "Christians" denied and still deny His divinity or humanity in one form or another. It is to be noted that Christ must be treated as a whole person, as one person. He is not a God and a man in a kind of dualistic being.

It is the joining together of the divine and human natures in one person that is the fact and the problem. Yet the very existence of Christ means that God is concerned with humanity and that man is related to God both as created and as redeemed. If Christ is God but not man, we need not much concern ourselves with Him in particular. If He is man but not God, well, He is just another dubious historical character who claimed to be what He could not have been. If He is *both* God and man, that makes all the difference.

It took several centuries for the Church, thinking back on the event in Bethlehem, on the Cross and Resurrection that happened to this Child later, to figure out a coherent, plausible way to explain it so that it would be intelligible and not contradictory to the human mind. Today, to deny this relation of man and God in Christ, one has to embrace a philosophy that does not allow for a relation between matter and spirit in a real world. In this sense, the Incarnation and nativity of this Christ was directed to the human mind at its best, to its thinking when its thinking is most in tune with *what is*.

Revelation was directed to everybody, to the simple, the ordinary, and the common folks of this world. But it was also directed, at the same time, to the depths of the human soul with its thinking and willing. It was not something designed to confound man's thinking or to confuse his head, but to enhance them, to make them more what they were intended to be. We should not be too surprised at this.

Whenever a new mother or father looks at a child begotten and born of them, they see there what is of them and their parents and grandparents. But they also see there something more than could be attributed just to themselves. After all, they did not and could not "plan" that this particular child they see before them would come about. They understand that some transcendent aspect of reality is also present in what is obviously also like them.

Christ's birth was different, as Mary and Joseph no doubt sensed, because the Child before them was at the origin of all things, including themselves. When we wonder whether Christ might have been born in Siberia or in Bali, we cannot forget that whoever is born, at any time or place, is born in the Word. This Word is before the foundation of the world, in which, ultimately, all things originate, including ourselves.

If we wish to find the origin of ourselves and of our own destiny, we cannot avoid this event that happened in the City of

David, "when the whole world was at peace." His parents were told at His birth that He was to be called Emmanuel, or "God with us." In the end, this presence in this world of its Creator is what Christmas is about.

"Let us rejoice and be glad."

Chapter 18

⟋

The Christmas Fire[20]

Several years ago, I was given a very handsome Platinum Press edition of *Stories for Christmas* by Charles Dickens (2007). This book has 478 pages, so Dickens had much to say about this wonderful, wonder-filled feast. I recall Chesterton saying somewhere that ceremony surrounding the English-speaking Christmas is practically invented by Dickens.

We Americans have, in addition to Dickens and Yule logs, elements of the Italian, Spanish, German, Polish, Slavic, Irish, and other traditions in our Christmas. We hear a lot about the decline of Christmas, the substitution of all sorts of things for the centrality of the Christ Child and what He means and is. We wonder, nonetheless, about the heart of Christmas, about its essence.

It does not take much reading in Dickens to arouse a Christmas mood in our souls. I have read somewhere, and have often experienced it myself, that simply reading the first lines of a novel or a short story is enough to set us off, to make us want to know

[20] Published in *Inside Catholic*, December 9, 2008.

what happens next. The "once upon a time" is often enough. We are beings who want to know the whole story.

So I found in this collection a Dickens tale called "The Poor Relation's Story." It is a Christmas scene, a nineteenth-century family gathering. The story begins: "He was very reluctant to take precedence of so many respected members of the family, by beginning the round of stories they were to relate as they sat in a goodly circle by *the Christmas fire*." The "he" in that passage is, of course, the "poor relative" of the title.

On Christmas, I suppose, not a few "Christmas fires" still burn among us. But I rather doubt that many a "round of stories" before "goodly circles" can still be found in the land. Yet, the mere reading of such a sentence keeps alive in our souls a tradition that we may not directly know. Belloc indeed said that often writing about what happened in our home county is almost the only way to preserve it as we knew it. We would be better off, I suspect, if, instead of watching television, we told one another "goodly stories" at Christmastide. I recall that one of the charms about the Tolkien yarns was precisely when, after a wonderful supper, all gathered in the great hall to hear the stories.

Is Christmas a "story," then? Certainly, much of the "once upon a time" element hovers about it. Most of us can narrate its central drama—the decree of Caesar Augustus, the manger in Bethlehem, the shepherds, the angels on high, peace on earth, goodwill to men, Joseph, Mary, the Child.

Two kinds of story exist: those about something that never happened and those about something that did. There is truth in both kinds. We are told by not a few exegetes that Christmas is but a story. What we read, the donkey and all that, never happened.

Yet the story, as it stands, is intelligible enough to us. We know there was a Roman census. Bethlehem, Jerusalem, and

Egypt were real places. Every detail of the Nativity narrative has been doubted by someone.

At Midnight Mass in St. Peter's Basilica in 2006, Benedict XVI said: "The Child lying in the manger is truly God's Son. God is not eternal solitude but rather a circle of love and mutual self-giving. He is Father, Son, and Holy Spirit." He is "true God and true man."

"Why is this important?" we might ask, the "who Christ is"? Not many people ask this question, I think. We have developed a protective habit of not asking important questions. We are pretty sure that the answers to the questions will not be to our liking. So we figure out other explanations, more comforting ones, as we like to think, though it is difficult to think of anything more comforting than the Nativity, in its truth.

If we think about it, it is not too difficult to believe in or understand the arguments that suggest that God exists. The real dividing line, even today, especially today, comes with the "who" of this Child in Bethlehem. The last lines of Romano Guardini's book *The Humanity of Christ* read:

> In the midst of creation in its sinful state, a center was born which the Son of God drew into His own being. It is there now—the starting-point of new life. This starting-point cannot be explained in terms of this world, but *its rays light up* the whole world. From this point the Logos reaches out and takes hold of the world, bit by bit—or else the world shuts itself up against Him, is thereby judged, and falls back into darkness.

These are solemn words among "men of goodwill."

The *Christmas fire*, the circle "gathered" around it, the tales, the "rays" of light: *God is not eternal solitude*. The Logos reaches out bit by bit. The world shuts itself against Him to create a "solitude" of its own that is not found in the Godhead. "The light shineth in darkness, and the darkness comprehended it not" (John 1:5, KJV).

We are beings who want to know the whole story.

Chapter 19

It Is "Bidden to Us"[21]

On the feast of Stephen, 1951, from St. Mary Magdalen College at Oxford, C. S. Lewis wrote a Latin letter to Don Giovanni Calabria, in Verona.[22] On this day after Christmas, Lewis invoked on Calabria "all spiritual and temporal blessings in the Lord" and added: "It is astonishing that sometimes we believe that we believe what, really, in our hearts, we do not believe."

At first, I thought that Lewis was telling us that he had some doubt about his faith.

Lewis's point, however, was something else.

We do not always grasp the depth of what it is we already believe. "For a long time," Lewis tells us, "I believed that I believed in the forgiveness of sins. But suddenly (on St. Mark's day) this truth appeared in my mind in so clear a light that I perceived that never before (and that after many confessions and absolutions) had I believed it with my whole heart." We distinguish between intellectual understanding and the overwhelming reality that our sins are actually forgiven. We can go

---

[21] Published in *Inside Catholic*, December 25, 2009.

[22] Letters published with a translation by St. Augustine's Press.

on acting as if they were not, a spirit, in fact, contrary to the meaning of faith.

Lewis then gives some advice to Calabria. "You write much about your own sins," he tells him. "Beware (permit me, my dearest Father, to say beware) lest humility should pass over into anxiety or sadness." I expected Lewis to say pass over into "pride," not into "anxiety or sadness."

Lewis had something else in mind. Some, on once being forgiven, think they will never sin again. But why are we not to be overly anxious or sad about even our forgiven sins? He cites Paul: "It is *bidden us* to 'rejoice and always rejoice' (Philippians 4:4). Jesus has cancelled the handwriting which was against us. Lift up our hearts!"

Never before had I seen that expression: "Jesus has cancelled the handwriting which was against us." The imagery is graphic, the list of our sins in the Book of Life. Even if this cancellation is true, however, we still can be "anxious" that we might not "really" be forgiven.

We doubt what is forgiven us. This power of forgiveness is what is new in the world. The ancients knew about sin and even about forgiveness. They just did not know who could really forgive. They did not really know the depth of sin. They did not know that its forgiveness took God Himself.

Christ came into the world "to forgive sins."

This power scandalized the Pharisees of all ages; or rather, it scandalized them because a man, Jesus, claimed it, a divine claim. This same claim often scandalizes us. We refuse to believe that our sins are so bad that they need a divine redeemer properly to deal with them. We think that we are insignificant. Thus, we can do what we want.

In 1947, Lewis wrote to Calabria: "Is it not a frightening truth that the free will of a bad man can resist the will of God? For

He has, after a fashion, restricted His own Omnipotence by the very fact of creating free creatures; and we read that the Lord was *not able* to do miracles in some places because people's faith was wanting." To sin requires free will. To accept repentance as a fact likewise requires free will.

How is our world different from the pagan world? In a letter to Calabria on St. Patrick's Day 1953, Lewis remarked that "they err who say 'the world is turning pagan again.' Would that it were!" It is becoming much worse. "'Post-Christian man' is not the same as 'pre-Christian man.'"

On September 15 of the same year, Lewis wrote that a good part of Europe has lost the faith. It is now in "a worse state than the one we were in before we received the Faith. For no one returns from Christianity to the same state he was in before Christianity, but into a worse state.... Faith perfects nature but faith lost corrupts nature. Therefore, many men of our time have lost not only the supernatural light but also the natural light which pagans possess."

If we want, at Christmastide, to understand Western culture, no one has said it better than Lewis in this passage.

Stephen, the first martyr, was stoned to death. On dying, he asked that his killers be forgiven. The scribes and the Pharisees responsible for Stephen's death freely rejected the revelation offered them. Stephen asked that their act not be held against them.

"Many men of our time have lost not only the supernatural light but also the natural light which pagans possess." Jesus canceled the handwriting that is against us. Let us accept it. Let us not be worrisome. Let us rejoice and be glad!

Chapter 20

⁀

Te Deum Laudamus[23]

On the last day of the year, in many religious houses, the community gathers for a solemn chanting of the famous sixth-century hymn Te Deum Laudamus ("We Praise Thee, God"). This hymn is recited in the Sunday and Feast Day Office of the Breviary after the Morning Readings. The hymn is in the common form of a thanksgiving prayer, but it is more than that, as it is primarily an act of pure praise. No doubt, at the end of a year, it is more than appropriate to reflect on what has occurred to us and to our world during the previous twelve months while we are doing what we are created for, to praise God.

The Te Deum is, as are all Christian praises, cast in the form of a Trinitarian unity. With its specific consideration of the Holy Spirit, the year 1998 ends one part of the preparation for the Jubilee of the Year 2000. The year 1999 is to be devoted to God the Father, and the year 2000 to the Trinity. The Holy Father has been remarkably concerned to call the world's attention to the central core of our Faith, which is nothing less than the knowledge of and worship of God. Somehow, I do not think

[23] Published in Crisis Magazine, December 1998.

the world, nor even the Church, has been quite prepared for the Holy Father's initiative.

The Te Deum Laudamus has been set to music by a great number of composers—Charpentier, Berlioz, Gounod, Purcell, Handel (five times!), Ralph Vaughn Williams, Gabrieli, Scarlatti, Verdi, Hayden, Bach, Mozart, and Bruckner. The authorship of the hymn is generally attributed to Nicetas of Remesiana, but St. Ambrose, St. Augustine, St. Hilary of Poitiers, and others have been designated over the centuries as possible authors. The old *Catholic Encyclopedia* says it is definitely written by St. Caesarius of Arles, though there are longer and shorter versions. It seems originally to have been written in Latin, not Greek, and to have been used liturgically in southern Gaul, Milan, and northern Italy.

The first two Latin phrases are "Te Deum laudamus; te Dominum confitemur." These are translated in the Breviary as "You are God; we praise you. You are the Lord; we acclaim you." The latter could say: "We confess that you are the Lord." The next verses are "You are the eternal Father; all creation worships you." Notice what is happening here. We have a hymn mostly intended to be sung—gloriously sung—but what it does is state what we hold God to be after the manner of praise. There is awe to the affirmation.

The next segment of the Te Deum refers to the praise of the angels, the Cherubim and Seraphim, who sing precisely "endless praise," as if that is their highest act. Not only is the Lord God of power and might "Holy, holy, holy," but Heaven and earth are "full" of His glory. Then the Apostles, the prophets, and the martyrs praise. The Church herself throughout the world "acclaims you Father." This is, of course, how God reveals Himself to us. Along with the Father is His Son, "worthy of all worship," and the Holy Spirit, "advocate and guide."

The hymn next addresses itself to the Son: "You, Christ, are the King of Glory, the eternal Son of the Father." This Christ became man "to set us free"; He did not "spurn" the Virgin's womb. The "sting" of death He overcame and opened "the kingdom of Heaven to all believers." These verses also are in the form of address and praise: "You, Christ" did these things. The present affirmation follows: Christ is now "seated at God's right hand in glory." We also believe that He will come again to be our judge. The final address is also to the Son—"Come, then, Lord, help your people." They were bought with "blood," Your blood. The final address is for ourselves, our completion, that we may be with "your saints."

The text says, "Bring us."

Why and where?

"To glory everlasting."

My old Book of Common Prayer contains an earlier English version of the Te Deum. It begins: "We praise thee, O God; we acknowledge thee to be the Lord. All the world doth worship thee, the Father Everlasting." And it ends, "O Lord, save thy people, and bless thine heritage. Govern them, and lift them up forever. Day by day we magnify thee; and we worship thy Name ever, world without end."

On reading these old English wordings, we are hard-pressed to think we have improved our language of worship, even while we marvel at that which this glorious hymn allows us to sing and recount, the praise we offer when we are shown the order of the divinity.

"We praise thee, O God."

Chapter 21

⌒

New Year's, 1740[24]

For Christmas, my friend Scott Walter presented me with a handsome two-volume set of *Johnsonian Miscellanies*. These were recollections and writings concerning Samuel Johnson brought together in 1785 by George Birkback Hill, himself an "Honorable Fellow of Pembroke College, Oxford and the Editor of *Boswell's Life of Johnson*." This edition was published in New York by Harper Brothers in 1897. Scott, one of my first Georgetown students, found them being discarded from the James V. Brown Library of Williamsport and Lycoming County, Pennsylvania. Unless it perchance has a second copy, any library downsizing by selling off anything of Johnson little deserves the noble name "library." It must have been a "No one has checked it out in years" decision.

The book's dedication is irresistible: "To the Reverend Bartholomew Price, D.D., F.R.S., F.R.A.S. (Fellow, Royal Society; Fellow, Royal Astronomical Society), Master of Pembroke College, Oxford, Sedleian Professor of Natural Philosophy, in Commemoration of His Long and Honorable Connection with that

---

[24] Published in *The Catholic Thing*, January 11, 2011.

'Little College' which Johnson loved, This Work Is Dedicated."
We need to recall that Johnson (1709–1784) entered Pembroke
College when he was nineteen.

The first section of volume 1 is entitled "Prayers and Medita-
tions." In this section are found "Prayers on New Year's Day."
The fifteen-line prayer for New Year's Day, 1740 (after which is
a cryptic note "after 3 a.m. in the morning"), begins:

> Almighty God, by whose will I was created, and by whose
> Providence I have been sustained, by whose mercy I
> have been called to the knowledge of my Redeemer,
> and by whose Grace whatever I have thought or acted
> acceptable by thee has been inspired and directed, grant,
> O Lord, that in reviewing my past life, I may recollect
> thy mercies to my preservation, in whatever state thou
> prepares for me, that in affliction I may remember how
> often I have been sustained, and in prosperity may know
> and confess from whose hand the blessing is received
> (no. 10, p. 9).

We don't say prayers like that anymore!

Prayer is addressed to God. We are individually willed, sustained, and given mercy. Why? So that we might have a knowledge of our Redeemer. Not being Pelagians, we do not do the
things acceptable to God inspired only by ourselves. On New
Year's Day, 1740, Johnson is thirty-one years old. He reviews his
life. Mercies are recalled that preserved him. A future state is
being prepared. If he receives affliction, he recalls that he was
also sustained. If he is in prosperity, he knows whence it came.
Prayer is also articulation and insight into our lives, into the
impossibility of our accounting for who and what we are by at-
tributing everything to ourselves.

New Year's, 1740

Johnson continues:

> Let me, O Lord, so remember my sins, that I may abolish them by true repentance, and so improve the year to which thou hast graciously extended my life, and all the years which thou shall yet allow me [there will be forty-four], that I may hourly become purer in thy sight; so that I may live in thy fear, and die in thy favor, and find mercy at the last day, for the sake of Jesus Christ. Amen.

On reading such a lovely prayer in our own language, we cannot but lament the almost forced dropping of the *thous*, *thys*, and *thees*. It was not an improvement. Again, Johnson asks the Lord to let him remember his sins. We usually do not spend too much time remembering them.

But why remember them? "To abolish them by true repentance." No other way can be found. Johnson takes seriously New Year's resolutions to improve our lives. Each year our life is "graciously" extended to us. Indeed, so are all the years of our lives.

Why more years?

To become, even hourly, purer in God's sight. The opposite is possible to us.

But why should we become purer each hour?

To "live in thy fear and die in thy favor."

Is this something "negative"?

Nothing is wrong with fear. We are not Kantians. Fear is given to us precisely so that we "die" in God's favor. We want "mercy at the last day." Pope Benedict XVI often told us to remember the words of the Creed, "He will come to judge the living and the dead." It is not a myth.

But we are to do all these things "for the sake of Jesus Christ." Even when we turn inward to our sins, we look outward to our redemption. To such petitions, we can say with Johnson simply, "Amen."

Such was the prayer of January 1, 1740.

Could we do any better on January 1, 2011? Why would we want to? Everything is already here—creation, providence, mercy, sin, repentance, remembrance, prayer, graciousness, thanksgiving—all "for the sake of Jesus Christ. Amen."

Part 2

From Ash Wednesday to Easter

Chapter 22

⌒

Ash Wednesday[25]

On Ash Wednesday, the Breviary cites Clement's *Epistle to the Corinthians*. Clement was the third pope after Peter, around the end of the first century of the Christian era. The First Canon of the Mass names him.

The letter begins: "Let us fix our attention on the blood of Christ and recognize how precious it is to God His Father, since it was shed for our salvation and brought the grace of repentance to all the world."

On Ash Wednesday, I like that line: the blood of Christ "brought the grace of repentance to *all the world*." Today the world does not much know about this bringing, or even want to know it. But without this grace, we are pretty boxed into ourselves. We live in a world full of sin. But no one wants to call sin by its correct name, lest it imply something to do with him, something to be done about it, other than to deny he ever did it.

The reason Christ's blood is "precious" in the Father's sight is not that the Godhead likes blood. It is because Christ's free sacrifice is what made it possible for the Father to offer to "all

[25] Published in *The Catholic Thing*, February 23, 2009.

the world" a way to repair or to repent their sins, one that would respect human freedom. God cannot forgive our sins by taking away our part in them.

God's way to deal with our sins requires something on our part, beginning with recognizing that we are, in fact, sinners, not just in the abstract, but in particular instances in our lives. We are, of course, less than delighted to hear about, let alone do something about, our sins. Indeed, today, almost everything conspires against our naming our sins or admitting the depths to which they disorder us and our world.

Yet, in the Gospels it says that God is happier over the repentance of one sinner than over ninety-nine just men. So, if there be so many, is the repentant sinner happy, not to mention the ninety-nine who have no immediate need?

St. Irenaeus (about A.D. 200), in his famous treatise *Against Heresies*, wrote: "The Son performs everything as a ministry to the Father, from beginning to end, and without the Son no one can know God." God, I think, was rather more insistent on our learning this truth than we admit. The urgency was to "go forth and teach all nations." Likewise, a strange, perhaps diabolical, resistance, is found against allowing this going forth to happen in the nations.

Basil the Great (d. 379) in his *Detailed Rules for Monks* — a great title! — wrote: "This is the definition of sin: the misuse of powers given us by God for doing good, a use contrary to God's commandments. On the other hand, the virtue that God asks of us is the use of the same powers based on a good conscience in accordance with God's command."

Sin is not possible unless it takes place in a being that is good, in one who seeks what he himself wants to define as good. To put it another way, every sin is a repetition of the sin of Adam and Eve, a choice, in each particular case, to define what sin is by ourselves. We exempt ourselves from the law of our nature, from the commandments that summarize it.

Especially from those who have the problem that (for their own good) repentance seeks to address, we hear that sin and repentance are too "negative." Tell us something "positive." This "positive" thing we want to hear, however, is something that enables us to be forgiven without our having to do anything. The fact is, no one can forgive sins but God alone, such is their de facto depth if we would only see it. The astonishing thing is not that we sin. We do not have to be geniuses to notice that this unpleasant activity happens rather frequently among us, however much we are reluctant to name it.

What about the "joy" over the repentant sinner that is echoed in Heaven? Repentance is not a cause of depression but, for most of us, almost the only source of our delight. What is this delight? St. Basil adds: "What, I ask, is more wonderful than the beauty of God? What thought is more pleasing and satisfying than God's mercy?... The radiance of the divine beauty is altogether beyond the power of words to describe."

On Ash Wednesday, it seems safe to say that we do not and cannot see such divine beauty unless we pass through the blood of the Cross. This is the way given by the Father to attain the real end that "all the world" seeks.

Chapter 23

≈

Lent[26]

"Let us, I say, consider who Christ is." These are words from Newman on Lent in one of his *Parochial and Plain Sermons* (VI, 5). He begins: "First, Christ is God: from eternity He was the Living and True God." Newman is not here giving his "opinion." He affirms what is handed down to us. The content was not invented by the Apostles or changed by their successors. It was received by them. They are reporters of what they heard. We are hearers of these words, about which, on reflection, we can make sense. If we are instructed to "do" anything about them, it is to pass them down, unchanged, to others.

In 1983, Walker Percy wrote *A Message in a Bottle*. Later, he gave a lecture entitled "Another Message in a Bottle." We can imagine these bottles floating up on our curious shores. What is the second message? "In every part of the world where novels have been written and read, the presiding ethos ... is that the salient truth of life is not the teaching of a great philosopher or the enlightenment of a great sage," Percy remarked.

[26] Published in *The Catholic Thing*, 2010.

The Reason for the Seasons

It is, rather, the belief that something bad has happened, an actual Event in historic time. Certainly, no one disagrees that the one great difference of Christianity is its claim — outrageous claim, many would say — that God actually entered historic time, first through His covenant with the Jews and then through the Incarnation (*Signposts in a Strange Land*, 365).

At bottom, the novel is how we deal with this event as it works its way into our own particular lives.

Lent concerns this "something bad" that happened "in historic time." Lent is a time during which we go back over the sequence of these historic events. They explain to us both that something bad happened in our midst, but also that some remedy is promised, anticipated, something that is gradually revealed at the end of Lent. Without the Incarnation this remedy could not have happened in the way it did. The Incarnation and the Nativity of an actual Person point to the Cross and the Resurrection of the same Person.

Lent is not the season "to be jolly," though it is not a time of sadness either. Rather, it makes us aware that we are involved in a mystery of disorder that passes through each of our souls. Many of us desperately seek to find a theory in philosophy, religion, or science to assure us that we are not in any way involved in this mess.

Thus, we hope, the spiritual remedies of repentance called to our attention during Lent are unnecessary to us. But this rationalization is just another way of repeating in our own souls the sin of our first parents. We want to construct our salvation, not to follow the one proposed to us, the one that will work. Christianity suggests that we pray and fast even to see that we need something already given to us as a remedy for the sins we do not like to acknowledge.

* * *

Newman gives a second "point of doctrine" that we need to "insist upon." This is how Newman puts it, following the first point that Christ is the "Living and True God": "While Our Lord is God, He is also the Son of God. We are apt … to say that He is God, *though* He is the Son of God, marveling at the mystery. But what to man is a mystery, to God is a cause. He is God, not *though*, but *because* He is the Son of God."

Christ is Son, Logos, Word.

Christ at no point "becomes" God as if He were not God from His nature within the Trinity. The basic mystery of Christ is not located in His Incarnation but in His life within the Godhead. He who comes into the world in the time of Caesar Augustus is already the Son of God from eternity. And He comes in the way He comes in order that our sins may be forgiven. Again, Lent is a period in which, looking back on these events, we become aware of the event we call the Fall. It is, if you will, the "big bang" of the fallen world.

But those who live Lent are not ignorant of the fact that this Son of God succeeded in the obedience that He showed to His Father. Christ was not a failure, even when the leaders of His time (and our time) failed to recognize Him as what He is, the Son of God. Lent is not a time that recalls the "failure" of God. It is a time in which men are to realize how they have failed to recognize what has been freely sent into the world for their salvation.

Chapter 24

⌒

Tuesday of Holy Week[27]

In today's Mass we read the account of Judas in John's Gospel. Judas is ever an upsetting character. He is not like Peter or the Good Thief, who did some rather nasty things but managed to repent of them. We are told that Judas later hanged himself after returning the thirty pieces of silver he had received from the chief priests. These acts are indications both of despair and of regret.

I have seen accounts suggesting that, even in hanging, Judas "could have" repented. "Who are we to judge?"

But no doubt Judas is a pretty sober case to think about. We wonder where each of us might have appeared in the Passion. We all have potential for terrible things to come out of our wills and souls. We deceive nobody but ourselves if we think otherwise. In the list of the Apostles, Judas is usually designated as the one who would "betray" Christ. And no doubt he did just that. Jesus tells him to do what he has to do "quickly."

We can but speculate on why Judas might betray Christ. He was chosen to be an Apostle, to follow Christ. He clearly was

---

[27] Published in *The Catholic Thing*, April 14, 2014.

clever. He had great potential as did the other Apostles, even though they were fishermen and ordinary workers. Apostles too have to accept and carry out their callings. I have never fully bought the idea that Judas acted because he was a thief or simply greedy, though he seems to have shown such tendencies. Not a few stories and novels in which Judas appears make him a disgruntled intellectual. He did carry the money. In Bethany, he objected to pouring the costly ointment on Christ's feet. It could have been "sold and given to the poor" (see Matt. 26:9). That remark itself smacks of an intellectual. It was at this point that Christ said that "the poor you will have always with you" (Matt. 26:11). More important things exist, but only if we have some sense of the transcendent order.

Yet, we know that the Christ was to be rejected by His people. Judas was a cog in this working out of Christ's death. Many people were involved. Yet, he who handed Christ over to Pilate had the greater sin (John 19:11). In the divine plan, all the figures involved in Christ's arrest, imprisonment, trial, and death were free agents. None of them "had" to do what he did. Whether any of them grasped that, before them, stood the Messiah or the Son of God in any technical sense is doubtful. But each one did know that he was dealing with a man who was innocent. Pilate even said so. Each knew that he had to lie, deceive, or fabricate to achieve what he wanted; namely, to have this man and His claim out of the way. One of the leaders, Gamaliel, later said that, if this work were of God, the opposition really could do nothing about it (Acts 5:39). He was right. They became agents who brought these events to completion.

When Judas left the room, Jesus continued His discourse. While Judas was still present, he heard these words: "My purpose here is the fulfillment of Scripture. He who partakes of bread with me has raised his hand against me. I tell you this now before it takes place so that when it takes place you will believe that *I am*" (see John 13:18–19). Christ begins again: "Now is the Son of Man glorified, and God is glorified in Him" (John 13:31). It is almost as if Judas's departure was necessary for the other Apostles to hear these things. Christ knew that the machinery of His death was in motion. It was His to face. His friends would flee or draw back. What took place was not confined to this Upper Room.

The first reading for this Mass is from Isaiah 49. "I will make you a light to the nations, that my salvation may reach the ends of the earth." One recalls again Christ's words: "My purpose here is the fulfillment of Scriptures." The writers of the New Testament wrote that this Scripture was, in fact, fulfilled in Christ's death and Resurrection. We are often puzzled about whether this "salvation" has "reached the ends of the earth." We know that knowledge of the event has reached all nations, though often restricted, rejected, or hampered. Perhaps "reaching" does not mean "accepting"?

Judas makes us think of the human obstacles thrown up before Christ's efforts. They become the occasion by which God's plan is carried out. It is rather eerie, certainly unsetting. Gamaliel's words seem exact: don't deal with these Apostles. "If it [their teachings] come from God, you will not be able to destroy them without fighting God himself" (see Acts 5:39). One wonders, on this Tuesday of Holy Week, whether this is not exactly what is going on today — this "fighting God."

Chapter 25

⌒

Holy Thursday: Political Life, Endless Life, and Eternal Life[28]

What would it really be like if we were to succeed, perhaps not in excluding death totally, but in postponing it indefinitely, in reaching an age of several hundred years? Would that be a good thing? Humanity would become extraordinarily old; there would be no more room for youth. Capacity for innovation would die, and endless life would be no paradise, if anything a condemnation.

—Pope Benedict XVI, Easter Vigil Homily, April 3, 2010

When the Lord rose from the dead, He put off the mortality of the flesh; His risen body was still the same body, but it was no longer subject to death.

—St. Augustine, Sermon on Octave of Easter

We distinguish life from death. The study of living things is different from the study of dead things. Moreover, different kinds of life can be identified. The vast majority of things have no life. Life is what moves itself to its own end. We generally distinguish between vegetative, sensory, and rational life. When all three of

---

[28] Published in *Ignatius Insight*, April 20, 2010.

these sorts of life belong together in one life, we call it human life. Man is the microcosm, the being in which all levels of being exist in an organized whole. Aristotle defined man in several ways, most memorably as a political animal and as a rational animal.

Man is a political animal because he is a rational animal. That is, he can move and be moved by his reason and will. He is a self-mover because he can think, will, and rule his members. He is a political animal, likewise, because he can speak and persuade. Force is not his only alternative. What is not himself, he can express in words. These words can be understood by others. As a result, man can speak the truth.

Every truth implies a relation to something else. In knowledge, that something else becomes ours, but after the manner of our way of being. The object we know does not change in our knowing, but we change because we know. We become both ourselves and what is not ourselves. Likewise, we are social beings who can laugh in all our relationships. We find lightsomeness about our existence.

In his homily at the Mass of the Lord's Supper, Benedict remarked: "Much to our surprise, we are told that life is knowledge. This means, first of all, that life is a relationship. No one has life from himself and only for himself. We have it from others and in a relationship with others." When I know something, I know that what I know is related to the thing that is known. I know *what it is*. And I also know that *what it is* is not something that I placed in it, but something I discovered already in it.

Much modern philosophy, doubting the connection of sense and intellect, has striven to eradicate any hint that some "substitute intelligence" can be found at the origin of even inert things. It denies the connection between things and mind because this assumption of a connection implies an intelligible cause. The origin of such a cause is neither in ourselves nor in the thing known. Though we exist in the world as intelligent beings, we do not give ourselves the power of intelligence. It comes with what we already are.

This awareness that we assume some human, natural, or divine order in things is what Nietzsche famously denied. He ultimately wanted to replace any thought of a divine intelligence with that of his own will. This denial implied, in fact, that no intelligence is found in things.

Modern thought had already eliminated this possibility of intelligence in nature, including human nature, by claiming, with Hume, that the "opposite of every matter of fact is possible."

It isn't, but that was the claim. That is, in such a view, anything that we encounter, as far as we know, could, at the same time, be something else. This position leaves us, in fact, with both an empty mind and an empty nature.

Nietzsche was logical in thinking that much modern thought left the world empty, waiting for something to be imposed on it. He was not wrong in thinking that anyone who really thought this way should conclude that God is dead. Whether "truth" and "spirit" are merely "prejudices" of the philosophers, as Nietzsche said, can be doubted once we have reflected on the possibility of the "I am the truth" passage in Scripture. It is not just another system overcoming the previous system down the ages.

In the title of these comments, I have referred to three kinds of life—political, endless, and eternal. All three of these lives are, in a way, related. This relationship is what I want briefly to spell out here. These considerations initially arise from the various homilies that Benedict XVI gave during the recent Holy Week. I am particularly struck by the initial passage that I cited above about endless life. Benedict had reflected on this result in

The Reason for the Seasons

modernity before, particularly in *Spe Salvi*. He points out that, even if we manage to prolong the life of an individual another two hundred or so years, such prolonged life will be mostly, to parody Hobbes, "nasty, brutish, and exceedingly long." It will be a life of indeterminate length beyond the fourscore years and ten. As Benedict says, such life will be more of a condemnation. It will itself be sterile and make everything sterile in the enormous effort it would take to keep it going.

Endless life in this world with nothing further, supposing we bring it about, has no natural purpose. It is "childless." Instead of replacing one generation with another through begetting and natural death, we keep everyone alive as long as possible. Since there is nothing else, death itself becomes the only evil, to be avoided at all costs. Our whole civilization has to be retooled to keep us alive on and on. But living is not just for staying alive: it's for living well and nobly. It's also for living for the highest things, which may not be in this life.

Death ends the natural life we are given. It does not end the transcendent life we are promised. With proper distinctions, death is both an evil and a blessing. It comes at the end of a longer or shorter development from conception, its beginning. It is given unto every man once to die, as Scripture says (Heb. 9:27). Benedict points out that death in this sense is both a relief and a punishment. It results from a sin in the origin of the being of our race, yet it is also a relief. It does not interfere with the purpose for which God created us, that is, eternal life.

* * *

What is political life? The civil society also has something immortal about it. It is designed to last longer than the lives of its members. All individual members of civil society are mortals.

The polity, like the cosmos itself and the species, were considered by the Greek thinkers from whom we derive our thought, to be immortal. The word meant "not subject to dying" because none of these things were in the category of substance. Each person will die in his due turn. But the relational order of the polity and the species keeps going, sustained by the new beings who continue to appear in the polity or species.

Indeed, though few do, political societies are designed to last down the ages. Something noble is found in this awareness of an inner-worldly immortality provided by the civil order. The laws, speech, buildings, literature, artifacts, and thought of existing peoples are carried beyond their actual lives. They are found in books, poems, films, statues, and song. These are passed on so that we know whence we came. Our monuments defy time. They are there to announce ourselves to the future and to teach the future what went before it.

Moreover, in the Greek sense, begetting itself was designed to enable a species to last forever within the world. It took so many individuals in each generation to keep the human species alive. The particular human species to which we belong has two ideas or realities here.

It must provide for an inner-worldly immortality. This is what the polity is really about, a place where the deeds and words of individuals can remain. The polity, as it were, is the playground of beings destined for eternal life. It is where they decide what they will be not in this world but in eternity.

Thus, the polity is also an arena in which immortality applies not just to the species but to the individual of this species. Each human being is neither body nor soul, but both combined in a whole without which the person is not what it is intended to be, a person. The existence of each person is not merely in a passing inner-worldly period, though while he is in the world, he bears the substance of the human reality.

* * *

"Everyone wants to have life. We long for a life which is authentic, complete, worthwhile, full of joy," Benedict said at the Mass of the Lord's Supper at St. John Lateran.

> This yearning for life coexists with a resistance to death, which nonetheless remains inescapable. When Jesus speaks about eternal life, He is referring to real and true life, a life worthy of being lived. He is not simply speaking about life after death. He is talking about authentic life, a life fully alive and thus not subject to death, yet one which can already, and indeed must, begin in this world.

Eternal life is not political life. Rather, political life is the scene in which human persons ordered to eternal life decide whether they will live it or reject it, whether they will be judged worthy of it or not.

At the Stations of the Cross at the Colosseum, Benedict said: "From the day on which Christ was raised upon it, the Cross, which had seemed to be a sign of desolation, of abandonment, and of failure, has become a new beginning. From the profundity of death is raised the promise of eternal life." Eternal life is not political life. It is not the life of the abstract species down the ages. It is not endless life with no death. It is the human being's ultimate gift, of living the inner life of the Godhead, the Trinitarian life.

Paradoxically, Nietzsche argued that if we abolish suffering and struggle, we will have to reinvent them, for they are the incentives that cause us to prosper in the world. He argues that suffering will have to be "willed" and chosen. He replaces fortune with his political will.

The Cross is, precisely, the same thing in a different mode.

It is different, however, in that Nietzsche can promise no escape from suffering, even if it has its uses: we can only understand and reenact its necessity.

Death was not God's will in the beginning. If we recall the story of our first parents, it was their and our will. But the kind of heroic life that Nietzsche envisions in this world is really not the life for which we exist.

We do not exist for the "eternal return." We exist for everlasting life.

In his *Urbi et Orbi* message on Easter Sunday, the pope said: "Easter is the true salvation of humanity!... Easter has reversed that trend. Christ's resurrection is a new creation.... It is an event that has profoundly changed the course of history." Christ's risen body, Augustine said, is no longer "subject to death." But it once was so subject because Christ was true God and true man.

The Resurrection is not an idea. It is not a theory. It is an event. That is, it is something that happened in history. We have witnesses for it. These witnesses tell us what they saw. This event changed the course of history. How so? It allowed us to escape endless death as an ideal and object of science. It allowed us to accept political life but not confuse it with the kind of life that is ultimately promised.

Almost all modern thought is a search for a substitute for the resurrection of the body that is promised to each of us. But the "true salvation of humanity" has already arrived. It has already changed the course of history.

What it has not done, however, and cannot do, is prevent those who reject it as the essential meaning of their very personal being from seeking for a this-worldly alternative to the Resurrection of Christ and the resurrection of the body.

There are only two secular ways to go: to an unending political future in this world that deifies the state or to a scientifically engineered endless life in this world for each human being afraid to die. Neither of these alternatives is worthy of us. This too is what Easter is about in light of the alternatives that man in his thought proposes to us.

Chapter 26

⁓

Good Friday[29]

The Breviary for Good Friday cites Hebrews 9:28: "Christ was offered up once to take away the sins of many; he will appear a second time not to take away sin but to bring salvation to those who eagerly await him."

These words bear a finality. Christ was offered up *once*. He was not offered up twice or thrice.

Offered up to whom?

To His Father.

Why?

That sins be taken away.

Are sins so serious that the Son of God must atone for them? Surely nothing we do is *that* important.

We underestimate our dignity. "Against whom we do sin" includes the Father. He has established our dignity from the beginning.

Moreover, Christ's being offered up had a purpose — "to take away the sins of many." We hear that Christ takes away *all* sins. But the formulation in Hebrews has its point. Christ came to

[29] Published in *The Catholic Thing*, April 2, 2010.

judge the living and the dead. Our sins are not taken away without our input. We too must acknowledge our own disorder. This acknowledgment cannot be forced. It must be free. One might say here that God is helpless against our will to resist Him. He will not violate His own laws placed in our being.

Christ will appear a second time.

Why?

To judge the living and the dead.

We accept the truth of this latter statement not because we see it, but because it forms part of the whole order in which the existence of Christ as a fact is established. The second time He will not "take away our sins." This judgment will already have been accomplished. We either choose to remain in them or seek their forgiveness from Him who alone can forgive.

We find an "eagerness" in the realization that sins are judged and forgiven. We are to receive "salvation."

What is this salvation?

It is the result of the alternate plan, as it were, that resulted from man's initial sin, his *original sin*, as it is called. God did not intend death and sin, though He did intend that the created person be invited to participate in His inner life. This participation was the reason for His initial creation. But the inner nature of the Godhead is such that no one can belong to it unless both invited and chosen. We often wonder about this because the chosenness involves our own response to the love in which we are initially created.

We were given, as it were, a second chance. But this second chance involved the Incarnation of the Second Person of the Trinity, the Logos. God will not coerce us to accept what He wants of us. Our love cannot be forced and still be what it is. It must be free.

Good Friday

The scene on Good Friday is both an atonement that we could not make by ourselves and a sign to us of how important our lives are. The Good Friday Veneration of the Cross contains this refrain: "Behold, the wood of the Cross on which hung our salvation."

We are to "behold."

Behold what?

"The wood of the Cross."

Why is this important?

Because our Savior hung there, suffering this terrible Roman form of execution. Yet many do not want to behold. They cannot accept this path as their "salvation." But it is the only one that anyone is offered, the one most in accord with our nature and condition.

A Good Friday antiphon reads: "We worship you Lord; we venerate your Cross; we praise your resurrection. Through the Cross you brought joy to the world."

This Cross evidently does not only refer to resurrection. It brings "joy" to the world.

What joy does it bring?

Certainly, the fact that after the Cross comes the Resurrection. It is a joy also to know that we are redeemed. Once we know this, we need not wander the world looking for an alternate salvation.

Nothing describes our world better than a place being torn asunder looking for a salvation other than this one, the one offered on the Cross. But it is offered, not commanded. We are treated so carefully. We cannot be saved if we will not cooperate in the grace given to us. All are saved in the Cross, but not all accept it.

No human drama is more important than this one. None tells us better what we are. None more respects our freedom to acknowledge it. The cost of rejection is to have only this world to ourselves. Hell is pictured as a punishment. But it is better understood as a dullness, a dullness that refuses to accept the joys that we are offered through the Cross.

Chapter 27

⁀

Holy Saturday: The World: "A Space for Knowledge and Truth"[30]

To say that God created light means that God created the world as a space for knowledge and truth, as a space for encounter and freedom, as a space for goodness and for love.

—Pope Benedict XVI, Homily, Easter Vigil, April 7, 2012

Benedict began his sermon at this year's Easter Vigil in St. Peter's Basilica with these brief propositions:

1. Easter is the "feast of the new creation."
2. "Jesus is risen and dies no more."
3. Jesus opens us to a "new life, one that no longer knows illness and death."
4. God "has taken mankind up into God himself."

We have a "new" creation contiguous with an "old" creation. Jesus, at a definite time and place, is risen. He will undergo no other death. This new life is beyond this life; it arises out of it, but only with God's grace. The intention of God is to associate men within the inner life of the Godhead. This "taking up" of

---

[30] Published in *Catholic World Report*, 2012.

man into the Trinitarian life is the original purpose of creation itself.

What has newly opened up for mankind is its possibility to live this inner life of God. It is made possible by the Incarnation, life, death, and Resurrection of Christ. "Creation has become greater and broader."

Reflecting this new creation, the Easter Liturgy begins with light. "Creation is presented as a whole that includes the phenomenon of time." The first six days of creation are ordered to the Seventh Day, when God rested. Time begins not with itself but with creation. Before creation only God's time, eternity, exists.

Creation is ordered to the coming together of the creatures God has brought forth from nothing. "The seven days are an image of completeness, unfolding in time," Pope Benedict said in his homily. "They are ordered towards the seventh day, the day of the freedom of all creatures for God and for one another. Creation is therefore also directed towards the coming together of God and His creatures; it exists so as to open up a space for the response to God's great glory, an encounter between love and freedom."

That is a remarkable passage. Creation has a direction. It is not created for itself alone. Something is to "unfold in time."

What is this?

All are ordered to the day of freedom both of God and of creatures.

God's creation is not a necessity of His being. It is a gift of His inner life, His Love, which is the essence of His inner life. The adventure of God, as it were, is freely given to be freely received.

By whom?

By us men.

The cosmos provides a "space" wherein we can "respond" to God's great glory. We must do this freely, in love.

* * *

The Easter Vigil is suffused with light. Genesis begins with the creation of light. Benedict notes that the sun and the moon are created not on the first day but on the fourth. Why is this? To prevent us from making them gods and goddesses, as the ancients were tempted to do. The light of God is the light of intelligence that suffuses the universe. The sun and the moon are creatures. "They are preceded by the light through which God's glory is reflected in the essence of the created thing." The essence of a created thing is that it exists; it exists as this kind of a thing. It did not cause itself to be.

Benedict next asks: "What is the creation account saying here?" It says that light "makes encounter possible." If we cannot see, we cannot meet except by chance. It makes "communication possible. It makes knowledge possible; it makes freedom and progress possible." Light and intelligence illuminate each other. Unless things are luminous, we cannot see them. If we cannot see them, we cannot know them. To see is directed to knowing.

Light, as Plato also saw, is an "expression of the good that both is and creates brightness." "Evil hides." "To say that God created light means that God created the world as a space for knowledge and truth, as a space for encounter and freedom." The world is a place where knowledge and truth can be mutually known. When we know the truth, when we see things, we want to meet others, to tell them of what we saw and know. We are to make truth known to one another.

Matter is not evil. We are not Manicheans, with a god of good and a god of evil. Evil does not come "from God-made things." Where does it come from then? "It comes into existence only through denial. It is a 'no.'" Evil arises from a free act that denies what should be there. This is what happens in the space of the cosmos, this drama of affirming—or denying—*what is*.

* * *

Easter bathes us in pure light. This light comes to us in baptism. "Through the sacrament of baptism and the profession of faith, the Lord has built a bridge across to us, through which the new day reaches us." Benedict combines the notion of the waters of baptism and a bridge from God to us. The early Church even called baptism "illumination."

Why would baptism be called "illumination?"

To use another image, "darkness poses a real threat to mankind." Man can "see and investigate tangible material things." What he cannot do, however, is to "see where the world is going or whence it comes." Nor can we see "where our own life is going." We often cannot or will not see "what is good and what is evil."

This darkness is "the real threat to our existence and to the world in general." "If God and moral values, the difference between good and evil, remain in darkness, then all other 'lights' that put incredible technical feats within our own reach, are progress but also dangers that put us and the world at risk."

We can light up our cities in such a way that the stars disappear from view. "With regard to material things, our knowledge and our technical accomplishments are legion, but what reaches beyond, the things of God and the question of good, we can no longer identify." The light of faith is offered to us to see the order of things that most concern us.

"God created the world as a space for knowledge and truth." "God has taken mankind up into God himself." "Creation exists to open a space for response to God's great glory."

Holy Saturday

Benedict has a genius that takes him to the heart of what we would know. To put our lives and world in order, we need to know what we are, why we exist. Our end transcends even our nature. We are taken up into God Himself. We can say no to this gift in the space wherein the drama of our existence is worked out. This is the other side of our freedom. Its positive side is that we can also say yes. What is not possible is that God Himself say our yes or no for us. All that is possible is for God to show us the light and to give us, in the Passion, an example of what our no means.

Chapter 28

⁓

Resurrection and Original Sin[31]

That something is wrong with human nature has been known since ancient times, in all cultures, by any individual who, like Augustine, reflects on himself, on his own life, in the clear honesty of his memory. But we must be accurate. Human nature as such seems to be intact. Human nature is good, but something seems disordered in the human condition in which we find ourselves to be born and in which we live, in all times and in all places. The account in Genesis does not allow us to hint that human nature itself is evil or corrupt. Yet, there is a tendency, a disorder that each of us can identify in our own souls, that makes it difficult to do what we ought.

A *New Yorker* cartoon puts us in a handsome New York apartment. A not-so-young but not-so-old couple are sitting after dinner in their living room. He is somewhat balding, settled quietly reading the paper. His wife is rather younger, quite pretty, obviously enthusiastic, and eager to meet any problem in herself or in the world. As her husband looks up with some perplexed astonishment, she informs him, brightly, "Dr. Stolner said it might

[31] Published in *Crisis Magazine*, April 1995.

be nice if I let you see my darker side." We might ask ourselves why is this funny?

Generally speaking, we know that we, like the young wife, might indeed have a darker side hidden away someplace. But it has generally been considered more appropriate to follow the advice exactly the opposite of that of this Dr. Stolner. That is, we should try rather to control, rule, subdue, if possible, our darker side. We should not do something wrong or sinful or disordered just so we can assure our husbands or our friends that we are just like anyone else. No doubt, any sensible husband will already know his wife's "darker side" after a few years of living with her. That we are, in practice, sinful creatures, that we do have a more unpleasant side of our characters, no one can really doubt.

In speaking of Augustine, Father Ernest Fortin has pointed out that the difference between Augustine as a Christian and the classical authors such as Plato and Aristotle is not about whether they had a common understanding of virtue and of happiness. They do, pretty much. If Christians do not wholly agree with the classical authors, it is not so much because these latter were wrong.

Rather, the disagreement is because the classical authors were incomplete or unable to guess how to resolve their difficulties in practicing the virtues. Christians, for the most part, recognized that man in his natural and unredeemed status would find it somehow quite difficult to practice virtue. The Christian theory of grace was simply a recognition that we needed more than ourselves—even at our best, even as philosophers—actually to practice virtue, even when we knew pretty much what it was.

The *Catechism of the Catholic Church* (388–389) teaches that understanding sin in its fullness requires revelation, even though Aristotle, for example, knew that in practice, there was some basic wickedness in human nature. Aristotle could also account for how we generally did wrong, when we did do something wrong. However, the ultimate meaning of the Fall was fully understood only in the light of the death and Resurrection of Christ. The execution of Christ, the Lamb of God, graphically cut through any suspicion that what we do is unserious and does not ultimately reach the Godhead.

The account of the Fall, the meaning of original sin, ought not, I think, to be looked upon as some sort of alien imposition, some sort of outmoded doctrine that each of us does not somehow encounter every day of our lives. Original sin is in many ways the most relevant of doctrines, the one we need above most others to understand ourselves, to explain ourselves to ourselves.

If I can put it this way, original sin is the foundation of our very dignity because it stands at the basis both of our freedom —our radical freedom and the risk it entails—and of our relation to others.

If I sin or do something wrong, what I do is my own fault, to be sure. Yet, since it is a real human thought or action that I do, it cannot avoid affecting others. We are bound together thus both in our virtues (in what we do that is right) and in our sins (in what we do that is wrong). Were it not so, we would live strange lives in absolute isolation from one another, both in virtue and in vice, which is clearly not the case.

"The doctrine of original sin is, so to speak, the reverse side of the Good News that Jesus Christ is savior of all men." The *Catechism* continues, "All need salvation, and that salvation is offered to all through Christ. The Church ... knows very well that we cannot tamper with the revelation of original sin without undermining the mystery of Christ" (389).

That is to say, the mystery of Christ, as we know it, as it is revealed to us not as we might like it to be, stands in the context of the Fall, of sin. Christ came into this world, in which we ourselves live, to redeem sinners. He did not come to make us feel good. He did not come to restructure society as if somehow this restructuring would solve the problem of our sinfulness in a way external to ourselves, to our wills. Christ came because of our darker sides, which are manifest in our sins.

Aristotle already knew that we could usually give a very good account of why we did something wrong. Indeed, this account is the first thing we do when we are confronted with our own wrongdoing. We explain, rationally, why we did what we did. It will often sound most plausible. Of course, we also suppress the whole story and limit ourselves to that part of it that justifies our deeds to others.

But the Christian revelation, that Christ came to save sinners, is intended to intensify our awareness of our actions, of their consequences, and of our need to acknowledge them in their very disorder. We need more than philosophical reasoning to do this. This need is why Christ came into the world, and, in so doing, He called us to something much more than we might otherwise have been able to expect. So, the revelation of the deep disorder of sin is, at the same time, in its remedy, also a revelation of our real destiny, something we could not anticipate, the Resurrection of Christ, the resurrection of the body.

John Paul II has been remarkably persistent in recalling to our attention the reality of original sin. He does not, like so many theologians, try to explain it away or minimize it. He sees quite clearly how important it is not merely as a kind of political doctrine that would remind us that even our politicians are sinners so that we should not put all our trust in them, but also as a doctrine about our human dignity. Thus, in *Centesimus Annus*, John Paul II remarked that mankind, created in freedom, bears within itself the wound of original sin, which constantly draws persons towards evil and puts them in need of redemption. Not only is this doctrine an integral part of Christian revelation; it also has great hermeneutical value in so far as it helps one to understand human reality. The human person tends towards good but is also capable of evil (25).

John Paul II's encyclical *Veritatis Splendor* is precisely the grounding of good and evil as themselves irreducible to each other. Redemption is not to be achieved by transforming what is evil into what is good, into insisting politically, personally, or culturally that we call what is evil good, or what is good evil.

Evil is not good and cannot be made to be. Redemption exists not to deny the distinction of good and evil, not to deny that we as sinners often choose what is evil. It exists to save us from what is, in fact, the real depths of the evil that we choose against the right order that God places in nature and in ourselves. Redemption exists to deny to us the self-justification that what we do becomes good on our own or on our polity's say-so.

In John Paul II's insightful book *Crossing the Threshold of Hope*, we find a passage about original sin that I have, since I first read it, often pondered. It is a passage that is remarkably subtle and illuminating about ourselves and about the disorders in the world that are, in fact, ultimately caused by original sin and its manifestation in our actual sins, in our efforts to justify ourselves in them. But what is most remarkable about this passage is its vivid awareness that behind the most serious sins, behind the external action in which they appear, which can be forgiven and perhaps repaired, there is something else, something that has to be called almost diabolical. John Paul II wrote soberly to this point:

Original sin is not only the violation of a positive command of God but also, and above all, a violation of the will of God as expressed in that command. Original sin, then, attempts to abolish fatherhood, destroying its rays that permeate the world, placing in doubt the truth about God who is Lord and leaving man only with a sense of the master-slave relationship. As a result, the Lord appears jealous of His power over the world and over man, and, consequently, man feels goaded to do battle against God.[32]

This is an extraordinary observation about original sin.

John Paul II places the issue exactly in our own pride, in our claim to be our own moral world. We ourselves are to make the distinction of good and evil; we do not discover or receive it. We can actually choose, therefore, to see things in a distorted fashion. We can choose to see God's world, which is given to us by a loving Father, to be rather an attack against our own self-constructed world. We can even see in our practical defiance a kind of haughty nobility in defending ourselves, in our own minds, against God Himself. We refuse to have any will but our own. We do see that, behind the commandments and the virtues that are given in our nature for our good, there is a will, a divine will. It is this divine will against which we rebel.

The resurrection of the body is, as it were, the Christian answer to original sin, to our own self-created world. What is behind the commands of God is the will of a Father who wants us, ultimately, to be precisely ourselves. We can be ourselves only if we understand and choose to be what we are, finite mortal

---

[32] John Paul II, *Crossing the Threshold of Hope* (New York: Alfred A. Knopf, 2005), 228.

beings, to whom has been given not only the grace to be virtuous, but the proper understanding of what God is like, of what
the will of God has decided for us.

God has decided that we shall rise as His Son rose.

He was sent among us to accuse the world of sin and to redeem us. God took the risk that we can choose against Him. But
He gave us eternal life, which includes the wholeness of what we
are, body and soul. This is the promise of the resurrection that
follows on the Resurrection of Christ, who alone enables us to
call God "Father" and whose will is there in the Word in all we
choose even as we choose against God.

Where sin abounds, grace abounds even more fully.

This basic Christian teaching is why original sin and the
Resurrection of Christ and of our bodies are related in a most
paradoxical manner. If we are "goaded to do battle against God,"
as the Holy Father observed, it is because we choose to see in
every rule and command, in every being, a word we did not make
ourselves.

We choose to be like gods, and thus we cannot see or receive
what it is that the Father has given to us. If we win the battle
that we fight against God, we are left with only ourselves. The
men who choose "to be like gods," to recall the account of the
Fall in Genesis, are those who are least like Him. Those who are
most like Him receive what they least expected, themselves, yea,
even unto the resurrection of their bodies.

Chapter 29

Resurrection[33]

In Acts 10:39–41, Peter tells Cornelius that "they killed Him [Christ] by hanging Him on a tree; yet three days afterward God raised Him to life and allowed Him to be seen, not by the whole people but only by certain witnesses God had chosen beforehand."

On reading this passage, the obvious question is: *How come?*

Why not reveal Him to everyone?

It seems "undemocratic."

On witnessing the event, would not anyone immediately believe?

Isn't this what God wanted?

Did not God make a tactical mistake?

We are not to doubt the wisdom of divine providence. But we can and ought to ask questions about what is told to us. Scripture, among other things, is designed to make us think. Every element of this passage from Acts, of course, bears scrutiny: Why the killing? Why the Cross? Why the Resurrection? Why three days? Why the being seen? Why by "certain" witness? Why chosen?

[33] Published in *Crisis Magazine*, April 2000.

The Reason for the Seasons

Why beforehand? Surely, God could have figured out a less complicated, more effective way to present Himself to mankind?

If we think long enough about the Resurrection, we begin to see a logic about it. A most peculiar thing about the Resurrection is that the principal objection to its truth is that it is what we would want if we could have it. The objection is not that it is not a good idea, but that it is impossible, even for God. Looking backward on the event, Christians rejoice in the "logic" that what they are, body and soul, will continue. They are not pure spirits, not nothing, not simply temporal. The Apostles' initial reaction to the Resurrection was surprise and skepticism. But through the testimony of a few men from that time, we can affirm that something happened that we simply cannot explain. At least, it happened once, when the Man who hung on the Cross was raised by God to life three days afterward. The Apostles give few explanations; they tell us what they saw.

Without this event, St. Paul tells us, our faith is in vain. How blunt this statement is! This Resurrection is not believable to most unthinking people. It is tough enough even if we have thought about it. But what is curious about it, what gives even the greatest doubter or skeptic pause, is its curious conformity to what we might want if we could have it. Nobody objects to the Resurrection because he can design a better ultimate status for us.

He can't.

The scientists who propose that we freeze ourselves so that, in a century, we can be thawed out, repaired, and set loose on the world advance what would in effect be an imitation resurrection, a monster. The ideas of reincarnation or eternal return are hardly better. If we keep coming back as turtles or philosophers, it simply means that we are not really ourselves, or that everyone is, eventually, us. The genius of the resurrection is that what remains, finally, is precisely us. We are indeed created to be and remain ourselves.

Someone told me recently, that if you see a family with a deformed or otherwise retarded child, you can assume that the family is Catholic, Mormon, or Pentecostal; otherwise the child would have been aborted before birth. All aborted children are created, from conception, for their resurrection. We can say that they will meet their killers if their killers manage to save their souls. But what is behind such abortions is the desire, fostered by pseudo-science, to produce only the "perfect" child. We even have talk of ordering your own child according to specifications from some genetic lab. The efforts to improve human begetting would be laughable, were they not so lethal. But the point is that all of this effort to produce perfect children and to let live only those who can have "useful" lives, is, if we think of it, a parody on the resurrection of the body. Long ago, it proposed that we shall indeed exist in the perfection in which we were conceived by the Godhead, in the Word made flesh in us.

In the end, God chose only a few witnesses to the Resurrection of Christ. What He had to say to everyone, to the democracy, as it were, was that each of you will be resurrected. But we can still choose not to believe in the Resurrection, because we must choose to save our souls in order that our resurrection be to life and not to punishment for our deeds. We can reject what we are given to be, even in our resurrection. God will resurrect each of us, but we still must choose Him. This even He cannot change.

Chapter 30

 ~

Resurrexit Sicut Dixit[34]

The Easter Antiphon, Regina Coeli, states that Christ "has risen, as He said." This phrase is remarkable. It is one thing, however astounding, to maintain that Christ arose from the dead. But it is another thing to add that Christ rose just as "He said" He would. Lazarus, for instance, did not know that Christ would bring him back to life for a spell. But Christ knew that He would rise, never to die again.

How did Christ know both of these things?

We cannot imagine, say, that on Easter morning, Christ rises, shakes off the wrappings, and says to Himself, "Goodness! Look, here I am again! What a surprise!" All the way through His public life we find references to the coming Resurrection: "Destroy this Temple [of His body] and, in three days, I will rise again" (see John 2:19).

The wording, "has risen, as He said," is reported in the antiphon itself. It is not a scriptural phrase from one of the evangelists. Rather, it is the report of witnesses after the fact. Such facts of our Faith do depend on witnesses.

---

[34] Published in *Inside Catholic*, April 4, 2010.

The Reason for the Seasons

What is a witness? He is not a philosopher or an intellectual who tells us his ideas or understanding about reality. Ideas and thoughts can be understood if we have the wit to grasp their point. They are universal.

Witnesses report not ideas but facts or words. Facts are events in time and place. They are seen by other human beings who did not deduce them from some theory but saw them happen at a given time and in a given place. St. Paul said that if Christ did not rise, our faith is in vain (see 1 Cor. 15:14). He was giving us a logical conclusion based on a fact that either he saw or he knew of others who saw. If the fact is not there, the theory that it might be nice or a good idea is, in effect, useless as proof that it happened.

Christianity is a religion bound together by witnesses to a fact. Our faith is not faith in faith. It is an acceptance of a testimony of someone who saw. Christianity is not a theory, though it is addressed to intelligence. Once we know what happened, we are to think about it, to examine whether it makes sense. We will find that this very examination is itself an impetus to philosophize about the depths of reality that we would not otherwise think about, had the witnesses not reported to us what they saw.

Friends of mine recently visited Nazareth, the home of Jesus and Mary, the place in which Christ grew up. Many people today will not allow us to use the word *Christ* to identify Jesus, because it is a "religious" word. But actually, it is a word that must also be used if we are to describe accurately what the witnesses saw. They saw a man who said: "Before Abraham was, I am" (John 8:58).

As my friends went into Nazareth, now with a significant Muslim presence, they saw, near the Christian basilica, the following banner in defiant English: "Allah alone is God and did not come into the world through means of some human betrothal." If read carefully, of course, in spite of the fact that the banner is meant to deny the Incarnation of the Son of God, it is true that God did not come into the world through any mere "human betrothal."

The Son of God, the Logos, however, did come into the world through Mary's acceptance of Gabriel's message to her, her "*Fiat mihi secundum verbum tuum*" (Be it done unto me according to thy word) (Luke 1:38). Without this response, the Incarnation and its sequence could not have happened as we know it and as the witnesses report it.

Once the Resurrection is reported to us as a fact, as witnessed in its effects by those who saw Christ, we realize that Christ did not appear to everyone, but to a few, maybe a couple of hundred or thousand, but the chief witnesses were those who knew Him. As with Thomas and the two men on the road to Emmaus, it took some time to identify this Christ, now seen, with the one who was crucified on Good Friday.

We put these things together: the Incarnation, the Cross, the Resurrection, the *Who* involved in this life of one Person. On reflection, we see it as a unified whole. These things did not just happen. They were foretold; they were witnessed; they were reflected back upon; they were reported to us. *Resurrexit sicut dixit*. This is the fact that makes all human life ultimately intelligible. Without this Resurrection, not only is our faith in vain, but our whole human reality is in vain.

Chapter 31

The Defiant Feast: "Destined to Live Forever"[35]

Wine is of such divinity that it refuses to change its name. It has
kept the same name since it was first pupped. . . . Mark my words,
you my readers who are destined to live forever: it will not change.

—Hilaire Belloc, *Places*

God raised up Jesus on the third day and granted that
He be seen, not by all, but only by such witnesses as
had been chosen beforehand by God—by us who ate
and drank with Him after He rose from the dead.[36]

—Acts 10:40–41

Easter is a defiant feast. At the tomb we hear it said, "You seek
Jesus of Nazareth, who was crucified. He has risen, he is not here"
(see Mark 16:6). And earlier, in words that were remembered
later, "Destroy this temple, and in three days I will raise it up"
(John 2:19). Those who remembered said that He was speaking
of "the temple of his body" (John 2:21). The risen Christ was
not seen by all, but only by those witnesses chosen beforehand

---

[35] Published in *Ignatius Insight*, April 6, 2006.
[36] Reading, Morning Prayer, Easter Sunday.

by God. Is this unjust, that all of us were not there? Or, in fact, are all of us there because of the witnesses chosen beforehand?

"Unless I see in his hands the print of the nails, and place my finger in the mark of the nails, and place my hand in his side, I will not believe" (John 20:25). The challenge of the man who said these defiant words was literally accepted. His only response when so confronted was: "My Lord and my God!" (John 20:28). He was told, almost as a reprimand, that those who did not need this direct evidence were "more blessed."

We wonder why.

Certainly, witnesses remain necessary. The account is not imaginary.

The greatest of the heresies is that this world is enough for us.

The second greatest of the heresies is that God could not have asked us to live in this world because it is so full of evil and imperfection, including our own. Therefore, there is no God.

Or is there yet another, even greater heresy? That we can by ourselves make a perfect world, a world created in defiance both of the natural order and of revelation's relation to it?

Is the "will to power" the only reality?

Are we subject only to ourselves?

It is easier to comprehend the Passion of Christ than to comprehend His Resurrection, although we cannot understand the one without the other. The alternative to the Resurrection is never to die in the first place, something evidently once offered to us.

Men misjudge when they think that the most difficult things to understand are "Why do we suffer?" and "Why do we die?"

No, the most difficult thing to comprehend is "Why do we know joy?" Ultimately, joy is closer to the heart of things. We do not cause it to be what it is.

The Defiant Feast: "Destined to Live Forever"

Belloc, in a whimsical moment, addresses his audience: "Mark my words, you my readers, who are destined to live forever." That is precisely who we are. Yes, this form of address does speak to what we are, to people who are destined to live forever. C. S. Lewis said somewhere that "you have never met a mere mortal." He did not mean that we are not "mortal," in the sense that we will not die, that we do not know that we die. Rather, he meant that we are not "merely" mortals. The light in our eyes is from eternity. Pure passingness is not what we are. In being really mortal, we are yet not merely mortal. As St. Thomas says, in a phrase that I love to cite, *Homo non proprie humanus, sed superhumanus est.* We were not created to be simply human beings, but something more than human from our very beginning, which beginning ultimately was not ours to set in motion.

In many places in the world we are not even allowed to speak of the Resurrection—in no public school, in no Muslim space, not in the land of the Great Wall, and only cautiously elsewhere, usually in restricted places, as quietly as possible. Some of the world's greatest music, to be sure, has been written because of this feast and what leads up to it. We think of St. Matthew's Passion, the "Sacred Head Surrounded," the Resurrection Symphony. Even when it is officially avoided, the Resurrection cannot be totally avoided.

* * *

Easter, as I say, is a defiant feast. The real reason to reject it, I often think, is not that it is not true, but that it is too good to be true. If Christ is not raised, Paul tells us, the rest of our faith is in vain—and probably everything else. The history of thought is filled with efforts to show why and how the Resurrection not only is not true on historical grounds but cannot be true on scientific or philosophical grounds. Yet it seems that every historical analysis of why it could not have happened seems to bring forth counter evidence that suggests that it just might have happened. Every scientific effort to show that it could not have happened leads to other scientific evidence that it perhaps could happen. Every philosophical argument against its logic leads to an expansion both of what we mean by logic and what we mean by philosophy. If one does not want to believe it, be he warned, it is a dangerous doctrine to investigate.

Even from earliest times, we have all sorts of efforts to explain the Resurrection in a different way. The leading Jews wanted to put up a guard so that the disciples, who in fact were in no condition to give the matter a second thought, would not steal the body away. So that was to be one explanation: somebody stole the body and hid it away, never to be found again. I believe that *The Da Vinci Code* has Christ managing to slip away to marry Mary of Magdala, no mean feat, but many want to believe it, whatever the evidence. One of the taunts against Christ was to come down from the Cross. Then everyone would "believe." All of these approaches are combinations of the same thought: we can explain the Resurrection by some other hypothesis. Of course, there can be a million plots that might be thought up, and have been thought up, by the literary mind for any fact, including this one.

But all these theories at least suggest that something objective must be explained, if only to be explained away. The Muslim theory that Christ was only a prophet, but not God—a theory whose implications we are reluctant to face head-on—simplifies the matter. If it is true, there is nothing to explain. Christ, then, died like other prophets, whatever the details. Others go in the direction that the "resurrection" was a kind of spiritual thing.

The Defiant Feast: "Destined to Live Forever"

The "empty tomb" tells us nothing. To be a Christian, it is said, we do not have to take the Resurrection of the body literally. We do not have to be burdened with all those impossible problems about how it happened. It was meant merely to lead us to lofty thoughts. We are to be, as it were, "uplifted" by the "spirit."

All such earnest and convoluted theories need not be seen in too bad a light. They are efforts to explain what supposedly cannot be believed or what cannot happen. They all suspect that the orthodox theory, in its correct form, had best not be allowed to be presented. Thus, the disciples imagined these things. The Resurrection was a psychological theory explained by a projection of some hidden desire. What the disciples saw was what they wanted to see; therefore, they thought that they saw it. So the theory goes, rehashed in a thousand ways.

But, of course, the actual account of the disciples shows us a group of men and women themselves just about as reluctant to believe that the Resurrection happened as the most inveterate skeptic. Without themselves checking things out, none of the disciples were ready to believe the reports that the women brought. And the leading lady of the story, Mary of Magdala herself, thought the risen Christ was the gardener, who according to The Da Vinci Code, she subsequently ran off with, presumably finding Him not dead. The women who were actually recorded, however, were just as surprised as the Apostles, if not more so, by what they saw.

However, to give them credit, the disciples, even under pressure, held firmly to the view that they saw what they saw. In Acts, to recall, they are called precisely "witnesses." That is, they testify to what they knew from their own experience. We may not believe them, but that is our problem. We would not want them to change their minds because we had some strange theory about knowledge or experience that deflected us from understanding or admitting the possibility of what they saw.

* * *

The Resurrection of the body, on examination, is more paradoxical than we might at first sight give it credit. It is said to prefigure our ultimate destiny, so we cannot look on it as merely something that happened on that distant Easter morn: "The Lord has risen indeed, and has appeared to Simon!" (Luke 24:34). One does not have to be a genius to understand that if this doctrine is true in even this one case, the one case is not likely to be the unique case. It is certainly not presented that way. Indeed, it is presented as the Word that was made flesh, suffered, died, was buried, and rose again. We too are made ultimately in this image, for this destiny, after our own manner. We do not become gods. The resurrection of the body is the great doctrine that we remain ourselves precisely forever.

Aristotle had remarked, in a rather prophetic statement, that we would not want our friend to be someone else. Nor would we ourselves want to be someone else, even if we could have all the riches and power of the world. I have never met a student who, when he read of these two remarks, ever doubted them for a moment. It seems obvious that the remaining of ourselves to be ourselves is at the bottom of the whole structure of what we are.

The resurrection of the body is likewise the denial of all those theories about reincarnation, whereby we are given a second and third and thousandth chance to come back to try again when we fail on earlier times around. These theories are efforts to solve the problem of justice and injustice, usually without a doctrine of forgiveness, though in Plato there is also a doctrine of forgiveness; that is, the one against whom we sin has to forgive us. Christianity solves this problem at a higher level, but in solving it, we remain ourselves, either in glory or in punishment. No one else becomes us, ever.

Ultimately, we are not merely "souls." Nor are we angels or bodies without immortal souls. We are and remain human beings, body and soul, one person, who and what we are. Needless to say, this is what we would want if we could have it.

Moreover, we have other Aristotelian problems that we need to address. Can we be friends with God? And do the loves that we have for other finite persons do what we want or think love can do: Do they last? Or are they merely passing, of no ultimate meaning?

How could we be "friends" with God?

Obviously, by ourselves, we cannot. But we are not the only innovators in the world. It might be possible for God to figure out a way to make this possible. What if God is not lonely? What if there is an inner and complete life in the Godhead? The teaching on the Trinity, of course, means precisely this, that God is Himself sufficient. He does not need anything but Himself, certainly not the world. He does not "need" us to be what He is. But if something besides God exists, it would have to exist from the divine abundance, out of kindness or love for what is not God. This is the spirit in which we exist.

The Incarnation of the Word, the Word made flesh, makes the possibility of being friends with God much more intelligible. If Christ, the Word, is true God and true man, then we could be His friends if He invites us and we respond. The gap between God and man is breeched.

Thus, the joy of Easter is itself connected with our understanding of both what we are and what we are given. We know even that in some sense what we are is given to us. We also know that there is a strange incompleteness even in our completeness.

If we think about the Resurrection on Easter morning, it becomes clear that it responds to many puzzles of our being. We can sympathize with those who seek to explain it away. But we do not have to follow them, for the attempt to explain what, in fact, it is, when spelled out, is much the more dramatic and, yes, more joyous enterprise.

Belloc was right. We are all indeed "destined to live forever," destined to live as the individual, personal beings we are created to be. The Resurrection of the body is defiant. And perhaps only if we see what it really "defies" will we see it for the glorious future that it is, for each of us, if we choose it.

The fact of the Resurrection does not destroy or obviate the fact of free will. The truth is that we must also choose to be what we are given to be. Christ was seen by those who "ate and drank with Him after He rose from the dead." Those who ate and drank — perhaps they drank Belloc's wine "which has kept its name from the first" — are witnesses, chosen beforehand. What is witnessed to is thus not an "idea" or an illusion or a fraud, but to something that was seen by men and women who, that Easter morn, did not expect to see it.

Chapter 32

⌒

Easter[37]

The enormous concentration of power now vested in the executive branch of our government, the effective lack of checks and balances, the cost of it all, sometimes make the truths of faith seem irrelevant. This sense of helplessness is exponentially increased for many when they realize that those who call themselves Catholics have played a central role in bringing about this increasing absolute rule among us. We might be somewhat consoled if this were a system imposed upon us by some alien or demonic power. But, at bottom, it is the result of free choices of presumably otherwise normal citizens. We also might console ourselves that it may not be as bad as it looks, were it not for the suspicion that it is, in fact, much worse. We just do not want to know.

Catholics could have prevented this radical political turning, but in fact many were and are supportive, indeed enthusiastically so. The key issues of the faith are no longer considered to be basic public issues. The teaching authority of the Church, even when it is clear, is ignored or relativized. We are encouraged

---

[37] Published in *Ignatius Insight*, April 4, 2010.

to "move on." Generally, this admonition means accepting or accommodating ourselves to what are now taken to be settled facts, no matter what they are. We are becoming like Jews and Christians in Muslim lands. If we politely agree to have no effect in the public order, if we submissively pay the taxes to support this new system, we will be allowed to survive after a fashion. We can have a private, not a public, presence.

Easter, the commemoration of the Resurrection of Christ, goes on, of course, no matter the social or political order in which we find ourselves. The teaching of Easter is needed if we would make ultimate sense of our lives. Intellectual history, in one sense, is a desperate effort to find a sensible alternative explanation to Christian revelation. The modern mind is, in a way, embarrassed that it has not come up with an alternative that makes as much ultimate sense as the Resurrection. But, of course, this teaching is the consequence of a fact that happened, not of our own making. We might, in some sense, say that it was prophesized to happen, but that does not change the astonishing fact.

Various theories are proposed to explain why the Resurrection "cannot" be true or cannot have happened. We have historical analyses that seek to demonstrate that Christ did not exist — or if He did, He was only human. The evidence of His Resurrection is called unreliable. The Apostles dreamed it up after the fact.

Then we have the scientific theories, all of which strive to prove that this doctrine is incoherent. It lacks evidence that can be repeated or tested in a laboratory.

We have psychological theories that reduce the objective order to wishes or dreams.

Volumes have been filled with endeavors to "prove" that this event could not have happened, did not happen, or may not happen.

The truth of the Resurrection is seen as a critique of the actual public order, which it is. The fact and teaching of the Resurrection of Christ and of our own as a result are, nonetheless, teachings independent of the historical time or place in which we now live. They belong to the order of things that happen whether we believe them or not. Nothing, no political or social order, will be more important than the understanding of our being that is implied in resurrection. This reality teaches us what each of us is. The Creed says that "we believe in the resurrection of the body and life everlasting."

We can rightly assume that the teaching of the resurrection of the body is a minority opinion. We can also suspect that few see any relation between how we live our lives and what this doctrine is about. It has been the abiding task of the teaching Church to relate doctrine to practice. Things will not go rightly if we do not live rightly. We will generally not live rightly if we do not think rightly.

We are given intelligence in order that we might understand what we are. We are given freedom in order that, understanding what we are, we might choose to be what we are. This combination of reason and liberty results in the possibility of our choosing to reject what we are.

Why would we reject what we are?

We would do it if we did not want to be what we are intended to be. We can only choose this rejection if we think we can come up with something better. We are inclined to think this way when we suspect that the kind of being and end that we are given interferes with something we think we want.

We will thus reject what we are in order to establish a way of life and explanation that depends on nothing but ourselves. "As man grows up and becomes emancipated, he wants to liberate himself from this submission and become free and adult, able to organize himself and make his own decisions, even thinking he can do without God," Benedict XVI observed. "Precisely this state is delicate and can lead to atheism, yet even this frequently conceals the need to discover God's true Face."[38]

Paradoxically, the rejection of God can be, in another sense, a seeking for the Face of God. The very rejection of God implies that we search for an alternative that includes the rejection of what is said to be the Christian God. This alternative will never be complete. The celebration of Easter always implies an understanding of what we are and of what the world is that makes more sense than the alternatives when we see them spelled out and lived out. The resurrection will seem preposterous until we think about it.

We might propose an alternate "creed." Thus, "I do not believe in God; He did not 'create' the heavens and the earth. Christ did not rise again. Man will not be raised again either. He will not be judged. He will complete his life at the end of his days, however it happens. Nothing will be heard of him again. His existence meant nothing to anybody, including to himself, or to a 'God.' His highest aspirations are to be left alone in the cosmos for the fleeting moments of his existence."

The resurrection of the body puts things together again. It restores our face to the Face of God we see in Christ. What strikes us about the Apostles, those curious men, was that after the Resurrection of Christ, they rushed to see, to hear, to touch. They even smelled the fish being grilled on the seashore. They tasted it. They did not begin from some theory. Whatever theory they

---

[38] *L'Osservatore Romano*, March 17, 2010.

may have had ahead of time, they doubted. Their own "theory" began with what they saw and heard.

We do not know the percentage of the human beings who will come into existence on this planet who are already dead, having been initially judged, awaiting the judgment that puts it all together. Christ will come to judge the living and the dead. He, having been crucified, died, was buried, and rose again. He told us that we were made to follow Him.

Nothing better has been proposed to us. It is not a myth. It is based on the fact that the Word became flesh and dwelt amongst us. Our minds keep coming back to this fact, if we would know what we are. The world is composed of those who know what they are and those who are afraid to know what they are if it involves even their own resurrection. Yet, in nothing else is there hope. This is what Easter is about.

Chapter 33

＝

God's Supreme Work[39]

In the Breviary's Sunday Night Prayer, the short Christian reflection introducing Psalm 4 is from St. Augustine. It reads:
"The Resurrection of Christ was God's supreme and wholly
marvelous work." Augustine did not say that the creation of
the cosmos, however marvelous, was God's highest work. He
does not even say that the Incarnation itself or the salvation
of mankind was God's supreme work. Why is the Resurrection
of Christ?

Suppose, for the sake of argument, that Christ, the Word,
became man, which He did. Further suppose that He lived and
died on this earth, which He did. In addition, imagine that He
was never raised from the dead in Jerusalem three days after
His execution. Yet, without this Resurrection, St. Paul says, our
faith is in vain. To conceive an order in which this Resurrection did not take place is possible. We would read the Gospels
without anything following the burial in the tomb. But with such
a supposition, it would be difficult to think of why there was an
Incarnation in the first place.

[39] Published in *Inside Catholic*, April 24, 2011.

The Reason for the Seasons

Not a few scholars over the centuries maintained that Christ never rose from the dead. He was a pretty nice guy, a bit deluded perhaps, but no resurrection. No philosophical or scientific grounds, they insisted, could be found for such an improbable event. Therefore, it did not happen. In the time of Christ, Jewish authorities heard rumors that Christ would rise again. They insisted that His body was carted off by desperate believers, never to be found. Thus, again, no resurrection happened.

Why is the Resurrection of Christ God's supreme work?

In the Tuesday of Easter Week Office, St. Basil explains that "When mankind was estranged from Him by disobedience, God our Savior made a plan for raising us from our fall and restoring us to friendship with himself. According to this plan, Christ came in the flesh, He showed us the gospel way of life, He suffered, died on the cross, was buried, and rose from the dead." The Resurrection was the culmination of a "plan." It did not just "happen." The "restoration of friendship" with God involved the Resurrection.

Again, why was Christ's Resurrection God's most wonderful work? If God could create the universe, surely it was a simple step to re-create it. Standard Catholic doctrine teaches that the risen Christ ascended into Heaven complete, body and soul, to be seated at the right hand of the Father.

The question of why the Resurrection of Christ is God's most wonderful work is directly related to John Paul II's Theology of the Body, to the very meaning of man in the world.

In one of his sermons, Leo the Great explains that Christ "did away with the everlasting character of death so as to make death a thing of time, not of eternity." In Ezekiel 18:32, we read that God takes no "pleasure" in the death of anyone. The Resurrection of Christ is God's most wondrous work because in

172

it we recognize the bridge between the finiteness of man's being and the permanence of the inner life, the Trinitarian life of the Godhead. It is this latter life for which we were initially created, nothing less.

Death becomes, with the Resurrection, a "thing in time."

Benedict XVI tells us in *Spe Salvi* that death is both a punishment and a blessing. It is a punishment for the sin of the first parents. We "inherit" it. That is, everyone lives in the consequences of the acts of others in an unending chain that goes back to the beginning. The divine "plan," however, indicates that God does not simply let things be. He responds. His response, ultimately, is the Resurrection of Christ.

The Resurrection of Christ followed His real death. In this He belongs to the sons of Adam. But His Resurrection is the greatest work of the Father. For in it, all things in Heaven and earth are restored in Christ. Death is a blessing. We are not, as many would have it, to go on and on in this world as if that is what we are created for. The Resurrection of Christ is the divine work that assures us that our end is nothing less than for each of us, if we will, to be whole before the Trinitarian God. No other alternative would be the real "work" of God.

Chapter 34

⌒

Easter Monday[40]

In the Breviary for Holy Saturday, we find an "Ancient Homily." I have always loved this reading. It begins:

> Something strange is happening—there is a great silence on earth today, *a great silence and stillness*. The whole earth keeps silent because the King is asleep. The earth trembled and is still because God has fallen asleep in the flesh and He has raised up all who have slept since the world began.

The earth turns in stillness. We think of all who "have slept since the world began." These are the dead who, during all these ages, have awaited the Resurrection.

In his *World of Silence*, Max Picard writes: "It is as though behind silence were the absolute word, to which, through silence, human language moves. It is as though the human word were sustained by the absolute word" (43). "There is a great silence." *Verbum caro factum est*. The human word is sustained by the Absolute Word.

---

[40] Published in *The Catholic Thing*, April 25, 2011.

The Reason for the Seasons

Two days later, the mood is strikingly different. The stillness is broken by the "Alleluia, Alleluia." The refrain becomes: "The Lord is risen!" The response again is "Alleluia." "This is the Day that the Lord hath made. Let us rejoice and be glad." Christ appeared first to Mary of Magdala, then to Peter and John, and later to the rest of the Apostles. Thomas was not there. He needed proof. Christ no longer "walked" the roads of Galilee and the streets of Jerusalem. Rather He "appeared" out of the silence of His death. He was there, truly risen, in the room with the Apostles.

The reading on Easter Monday is from Peter's First Letter:

This is the salvation which the prophets carefully searched out and examined. They prophesied the divine favor that was destined to be yours. They investigated the times and the circumstances which the Spirit of Christ within them was pointing to, for He predicted the sufferings destined for Christ and the glories that would follow (1:10–11).

Looking back on the event of the Resurrection, Peter sees that it was anticipated all along, almost as if to say that the Resurrection needed to be understood as the culmination of a preparation, an expectation out of the stillness. The prophets "searched out and examined." They did not take things for granted. Perhaps the Apostles should have suspected. But they didn't. Once the fact happened, it was easier to see that this event was prepared for. It was not just a sudden accident with no before or after meaning or context.

Melito of Sardis writes in his homily on Easter Monday: "Both the Law and the Word came first from Zion and Jerusalem, but now the Law has given place to the Word, the old and the new.

The commandment has become grace, the type a reality. The lamb has become a Son, the sheep a man, and man, God." Creation and redemption have an order.

The constant Easter refrain repeats: "This is the day the Lord hath made; let us rejoice and be glad." We add "Alleluia." "Praise the Lord."

Why do we do this?

Why do we praise such a fact?

On Easter Monday, we also read in the midmorning prayer, "I saw the Son of Man, who said to me: I am the First and the Last and the One who lives. Once I was dead but now I live—forever and ever" (Rev. 1:17–18).

In the March 31, 1945, *Tablet* of London, Monsignor Ronald Knox wrote a short reflection on Easter. "Immediately after His [Christ's] death," Knox wrote, "His followers began to spread throughout the world, living a life of self-discipline and, where need arose, of heroic self-sacrifice, in the unquestioning hope that they, too, would be counted worthy of this Resurrection which they had seen and handled in His flesh. He did not simply convince men that He had risen; He convinced them that they would rise." Much of the world, no doubt, is yet to be "convinced." It is not so much that the fact is not there, but that we are reluctant to "search out and examine." The obstacles to belief are mostly man-made and man-chosen.

On Easter Sunday, Samuel Johnson was wont to record his annual Easter Prayer. Easter Sunday in 1781 fell on April 15. Johnson said that he "went early to church and before service read the prayer for the Church Militant. I commended my friends, as I have formerly done. I was one of the last that communicated. When I came home I was hindered by visitants; but found time to pray before dinner. God send thy blessing upon me."

The Reason for the Seasons

On the following day, Easter Monday, Johnson simply adds: "This day I repeated my prayer, and hope to be heard."

It is difficult to do better than that on an Easter Monday.

Chapter 35

༝

Easter Tuesday[41]

The Breviary's second reading for Easter Tuesday is the only citation in it of St. Anastasius of Antioch (d. 700). Anastasius was the abbot of the famous St. Catherine's Monastery in Sinai. Like Benedict XVI, he was concerned with the teachings and events of the Old Testament, with how they lead to those of the New Testament. "Christ ... has shown by His words and actions that He was truly God and Lord of the universe." Yet He was given over to be crucified. "Scripture also affirmed that these things were going to happen to one who was immortal and incapable of suffering because He was God." Just how these seemingly contradictory truths were both true was indicated by the Incarnation. This explanation involved another look at the inner life of God.

This "other look" is open to us when we read Christ's explanation of Himself. He never tells us that He sends Himself. Nor does He decide by Himself to come into the world. This statement means that He is Himself beyond the world. He is always "sent." He does say that He and the Father are one. He does speak of

---

[41] Published in *The Catholic Thing*, April 2, 2013.

sending the Holy Spirit. He identifies Himself as God, yet not as God the Father, the origin. He does tell us that He knows all things that are the Father's. This way of putting it means that reality is not only composed of the Father but includes the Father's "being known," hence a knower who can know the Father. Christ tells Philip, "He who sees me sees the Father" (John 14:9). He "sees" the Father. He is not the Father, nor is He the Spirit. But He knows both. He is one with them, God.

When St. Athanasius tells us that God has also suffered, he is careful not to affirm that the Father "suffers," except perhaps through the love of His Son. When we come to Easter Morning, to the "days" of Easter, we deal with the Resurrection of Christ. Christ the Word is likewise immortal. If Christ suffers, as He does, He must suffer because He is Word made flesh. We are asked to distinguish, to think clearly. So we affirm that this Christ is "true God and true man" without confusing the two natures into a sort of confused mixture.

Why do we need to know these things about God, about the Word, about the Spirit? Our knowledge of them begins in belief, in the trust that what is said makes sense. If we are told, say, that God "suffers," we are not simply to reply that God cannot suffer. Rather, we are asked whether any way exists in which the propositions that God cannot suffer and that God does suffer can be reconciled. The whole burden of early Christology demonstrates its possibility. We think on a new basis. We may need new philosophical categories that we did not see before.

Thinking about what has been revealed to us about God, about each of the three Persons, causes us to deepen our ideas about what a person is, about what nature is. We become more philosophical because we believe. Grace builds on nature, Aquinas tells us. But he adds that nature is more known and fundamental. When we are graced, we do not become gods or angels. We remain human persons with the peculiar destiny God has spelled out for us.

How does this reflection relate to the resurrection of the body? St. Paul tells us that, without the Resurrection, our faith is in vain. Why so? The first step is to show that the Resurrection of Christ did happen. The second step asks: "What does it mean?" "Why was it necessary or advisable?" The resurrection of the body means, if true, that the world is populated also by beings who are not gods, but who are nonetheless real and, in fact, immortal.

But they are not just "immortal souls" but full human persons, body and soul. The logic is impeccable. Man does not live by logic alone, but it helps. Why? We read in the Old Testament that God did not originally intend for us to die. We wonder: "Why, then, did not God just restore us to our original status?" The Resurrection obviously means that we still die. It also means that the unity of body and soul that was lost is restored. God evidently intends to carry out His plan for man, even if man initially or finally rejects it. Why? Because He loves the whole of that which is man. This love includes our free will and our bodies. The resurrection will restore our bodies. But not even God can force us to love Him. The only thing He can do is to indicate how much He loves us. This is what the Crucifixion is about. This is what Easter is about.

Chapter 36

On the Limits of the Divine Mercy[42]

It could be said that human history is marked from the very
beginning by the limit God the Creator places upon evil.[43]

Later, when the war was over, I thought to myself the Lord
God allowed Nazism twelve years of existence, and after
twelve years the system collapsed. Evidently this was the limit
imposed by Divine Providence upon that sort of folly.[44]

— Pope John Paul II

John Paul II was beatified on the feast of the Divine Mercy in
May. In his reflection on "The Mystery of Mercy," John Paul
II wrote: "It is as if Christ had wanted to reveal that the limit
imposed upon evil, of which man is both perpetrator and victim,
is ultimately the Divine Mercy."[45] John Paul had lived through

---

[42] Published in *Ignatius Insight*, February 25, 2011.
[43] John Paul II, "Redemption as the Divine Limit Imposed upon
Evil," in *Memory and Identity* (New York: Rizzoli, 2005), 38.
[44] John Paul II, "The Limit Imposed on Evil in European History,"
in ibid., 14.
[45] Ibid., 55.

the two great totalitarian experiences of the twentieth century, now becoming vague memories for most of us. Yet he could not help but want to know, if he could, why God allowed such terrible things to happen. Not a few use these evils as reasons not to believe or to claim that God is not good. But John Paul used them rather as an occasion to reflect on what God was teaching us by allowing them to happen, with, of course, the free cooperation of the men who carried them out.

In a famous passage, Augustine said that God never allows evil unless some good can result through its occurrence. He does not "cause" it but allows it. The persistent question that most of us have, however, has to do with God's "relation" to evil. We want to "blame" Him, not ourselves. Thus, if evil exists in the world, as most will recognize that it does, we must, to explain it, involve God in the whole mess. This approach would leave us innocent. We shift the blame to God.

John Paul comes at the question of evil through the perspective of the Divine Mercy, a teaching of the Polish nun Sister Faustina, whom John Paul admired. Benedict will later explain in *Spe Salvi* that the Divine Mercy has to be properly related to divine justice, to judgment. A world of justice alone is barren and cold. A world of mercy alone tends to accept everything. Both are necessary. But they do not replace each other.

The first section of Pope Wojtyla's little book *Memory and Identity: Conversations at the Dawn of a Millennium* is entitled "The Limit Imposed upon Evil." The very first thing we notice on reading this title is that evil is not absolutely unlimited. More broadly, no "absolute" evil exists. Nor is evil a "thing." Evil always exists in what is good. Evil has its limits, however extensive its presence may seem. God, in other words, will not simply eradicate evil from the world. The possibility of evil is contingent on the possibility of freedom and love.

* * *

We must keep certain distinctions in mind. The first is that, if only God existed, no evil would exist. So, had God wanted to eliminate evil, all He had to do was not create anything. But He did create beings that could choose against Him. Any other kind would not be worth having.

He did not create in order that they would so choose. He created that they would not. But He also created them to be free. He did not create automata that had no choice. He created them free because He wanted them freely to love Him. If they "had" to love Him, the whole effort would have been worthless.

So evil has something to do with creation.

The Manichean heresy, against which, in principle, Genesis was written, held that two gods existed, one of good and one of evil. The good god created spirit, and the bad god created matter. Genesis rejected such a position. It held that all things were good in their creation, including material things. Evil is thus not a created "thing."

What is evil, then?

Some people want to identify it with suffering. They want to "withdraw" from a world that includes suffering. Suffering normally, however, is a sign that something is wrong in a real world. If we never suffered, we would not know what is wrong with us when we are sick. Suffering is a kind of map that indicates where something is wrong.

Moreover, suffering is not directly a moral evil. Suffering can be endured. As Socrates said, "It is better to suffer evil than to do it." This principle means that worse things than suffering exist.

The Reason for the Seasons

The virtue of courage is designed to help us face suffering and pain, to endure them. Indeed, suffering has a redemptive aspect. Since Christ, suffering can be endured for the good and for the sins of others in union with His sacrifice. He too taught us that suffering is not the worst evil.

Suffering happens when something goes wrong. This consequence means that suffering happens in beings that are good but not perfect in their own order. Suffering is not the real evil. The most basic evil is not in the physical order. We attribute evil, for example, to the devils, who were once spirits of high intelligence. They could not suffer physical evils because they lacked bodies. But evidently, they could choose to do evil things. The evil that the fallen angels do is similar to the sin of Adam and Eve. Evil formally resides in beings that have free will, human or angelic.

Evil thus is not a thing but the lack of a good in a being in which what is lacking should be present. But what John Paul II wanted to know was whether evil had any limits. In speaking of the difference between the suffering in Eastern Europe and in Western Europe during World War II, the pope thought that God allowed greater suffering in the East. The people there were more prepared to face it than were those in the West. It is an application of St. Paul's principle that God would not ask more of us than we can endure. We remember the spiritual principle that God chastises those He loves, not because He somehow enjoys it but because He asks sacrifices of those He loves for the good of others.

* * *

John Paul II argues that the limits of evil are defined by the Divine Mercy. What does this mean? The implication is not that everyone is automatically saved by the Divine Mercy that will excuse every sin. It won't. It will forgive every sin that can be forgiven, but that is the point. Forgiveness is contingent on repentance. What was new in the world as a result of the Incarnation was precisely that sins were forgiven in principle by the sacrifice of Christ. Since He was both God and man, He alone bridged the gap of the heinousness of sin.

In the classic idea of punishment that we find in Plato and Aristotle, we find that the purpose of punishment, particularly voluntary punishment, was to restore the order that we have disrupted with our sins. Plato even tells us that we should want to be punished, that we are incomplete without it. Voluntary punishment is a sign that we recognize our part in putting disorder into the world. Plato also held that if we commit a crime against someone, it could be forgiven only by the one against whom the crime or sin was committed. What Christianity adds to this principle is that every sin is also an offense against God. This is why we cannot restore the order by ourselves.

Christianity combines both of these points. The sacrifice of Christ atones for the offense against God, and the public acknowledgment restores the validity of the law we voluntarily broke. Moreover, our sins can be forgiven by God and we can suffer the punishment, but the one against whom we sinned may still not forgive us. This refusal, however, is not our problem. The willingness to forgive is also included in revelation as one of our own responsibilities.

The limits of the Divine Mercy, then, are what God can forgive. He cannot forgive what is not asked or acknowledged. If He "imposed" forgiveness on us, we would cease to be free. This would negate the whole drama of our freedom and its consequences. God can respond to evil with good, as can we. Divine Mercy broadens the scope of God's relation to us. But that broadening includes the redemption on the Cross. God responded to the first human disorder initially by driving Adam and Eve out of Paradise. They lost the initial way to God that was offered to them. But they were promised and finally given a second way, one that still respected their freedom and let the consequences of their acts remain in effect.

The limits of the Divine Mercy, then, are established by what even God cannot do. He cannot make us free and then make us unfree. What He can do is make us free and, when we abuse our freedom, offer us a way to restore the law or the love that we have violated. But even here, it is up to us. God can give us an example of what our sins cost. But He cannot make us see it or admit our part in it.

Would it have been better, then, for God not to have created us? By no means. God indeed risked something in creating free beings. He risked that some would reject His love. But He paid this price. We are redeemed in a fallen world in which justice remains alongside mercy. God preferred something rather than nothing. This is the reason we exist with the offering to us of eternal life, if we respond to His invitation. Such is the drama of the world we live in. We are the risk of God. Those who re-fuse the gift of grace, however many there be, are left with their choice. God cannot take that away from them. This is the limit of the Divine Mercy.

Part 3

From the Ascension to Pentecost

Chapter 37

The Ascension[46]

Thinking of the feast of the Ascension, my mind goes back to the scene itself as described in Matthew. After declaring that "all authority in heaven and on earth has been given to me," Christ continues: "Go therefore and make disciples of all nations, baptizing them in the name of the Father and of the Son and of the Holy Spirit" (Matt. 28:18–19). Here, we find something to do, something to teach or know, someone to know it, and some place to direct our efforts—namely, everywhere.

We know, however, that a nation as such cannot be "baptized," only individual persons in a nation. A nation is not a person. It may last for some centuries, but it is not itself a substance capable of eternal life, as persons are.

This command and mission puts something new in the world. Previously, although knowledge was universal, most nations did not "convert" others. They wiped them out or subjected them.

This "going forth" mission (sending) has been imitated in a secularized form by Islam, communism, Eastern religions, and even recently by modern atheists. Every man's "truth" should be

[46] Published in *The Catholic Thing*, May 19, 2010.

that of everyone else. What is new in the Ascension is a charge combining action and knowledge. Something exists that, in whatever age or place, everyone should know about and should add to his way of life for his own genuine good.

Yet people are to be "taught," not coerced or hounded. So this "going forth" presupposes a willingness to listen, itself a virtue. It also presupposes a natural-law operative in every person that incites him to want to know the truth of things.

The Ascension message meets a natural desire in each human heart to know the highest truths about how to live. As Plato and Aristotle often intimated, perhaps the proper way to know and worship God might be revealed to them through what they "prayed for," though they could not imagine how. The "how" was what was "new."

Scripture and experience, no doubt, are quite realistic here. They warn us that opposition will greet these efforts to make the truths of Christ known to the nations. This is the historical record. Political force will prevent the change represented by the words. The modern language of "rights" and "dignity," moreover, develops a rhetoric of being free from such unwanted hounding. We will not listen except on our own terms, to our own "truths."

Under the present rubric of multiculturalism or relativism, laws and customs are now in place, even in democratic societies, that restrain this "evangelization." It is "proselytism." It is as dangerous to civil peace as the Athenian fathers saw Socrates to be to its existing public order. I do not want to be talked to except with my permission and on my grounds. My "right to exclude" is just waiting for some arbitrary judge to formalize it. We will be sued for "evangelizing," that is, for stating what is revealed as true. Law schools will teach this opinion as doctrine.

Socrates rightly did not want the carousing of the gods to corrupt the youth. We protect children, even from their parents. Nor do we allow much adult "debate" except among equally qualified representatives on both sides. We reach a final dead end wherein no one is allowed to talk about anything serious on the grounds that it will "offend" someone. We can talk of anything but what is the meaning of life or whether Christ ascended into Heaven.

Articles of civil peace, as Hobbes taught, require the force of law and opinion to protect us from such unseemly notions as Christianity proposes to be believed. China and Muslim states are already masters of this closing off of their society from anything untoward that does not correspond to what is legally allowed to be heard. Europe and America are not far behind.

The Holy Father recently spoke of the possibilities of bypassing these obstacles by the digital world. Yet, we hear every day of entities such as Google and other systems being subject to pressure not to allow certain critiques. We know that China has made this interference a major industry.

The Ascension: whatever else we know pales in comparison with what we need to know, which is precisely what the Apostles were sent to teach.

Most persons in most nations still do not know it.

Chapter 38

The Holy Spirit[47]

The feast of Pentecost closes the Lenten and Easter cycle of the Liturgical Year. The forty days of Lent, the forty days to the Ascension, and the ten days to Pentecost constitute the Church's yearly renewal of the mysteries of the Passion, Crucifixion, Resurrection, Ascension, and the Coming of the Holy Spirit.

Christian prayer is distinctive. We pray first and always to the Father through His Son, Jesus Christ, and in the unity of the Holy Spirit. When we address God in His fullness and properly pronounce His reality, we always find the Three Divine Persons, the one God. We address God in this way not because of some philosophical conclusions but because we were taught to pray this way by Christ. We find on reflection that these revealed truths about God lead to profound reflections on *what is*.

In Scripture, we find the Father. What we know of the Father, we know through His Son. "He who has seen me has seen the Father" (John 14:9). The Holy Spirit is less clear to us. His

[47] Published in *The Catholic Thing*, 2011.

personal reality is difficult to imagine. Scripture speaks of "fire" and "wind."

The Holy Spirit is also referred to as the Comforter, the Advocate. The Holy Spirit is the end or completion of the Godhead, the three persons in one God, fully contained in the divine reality. Nothing else is needed. When asked His name, God said it is "I AM."

If something else exists, as it obviously does, it does so after the manner of "love" and "gift," words associated with the Holy Spirit. What exists outside of God is love and gift, not necessity.

Christianity is accused of being too complicated for most folks. This business of three Persons, two natures, and one God seems in need of simplification. The Jews and the Muslims do not bother with these differences. But we Catholics do "bother" about them because we must. We are not concocting God after our own image or as a product of what we would do if we were God.

We have one basic duty.

We are to know and keep what is handed down to us from the beginning. God evidently did not say to us: "Look, I am only going to reveal to you what you can easily understand about me." Rather He said something like: "What I reveal to you in Christ, I want you also to think about. It will make sense and answer many questions that would otherwise remain obscure to you."

In his encyclical on the Holy Spirit, John Paul II wrote:

> The supreme and most complete revelation of God to humanity is Jesus Christ himself, and the witness of the Spirit inspires, guarantees, and convalidates the faithful transmission of this revelation in the preaching and writing of the Apostles, while the witness of the Apostles

ensures its human expression in the Church and in the history of humanity.[48]

Thus, what Christ essentially taught to the Apostles is what we hold today in the Church. Christ's sending of the Advocate was the sign of the Father's abiding concern that the purpose of His creation and redemption of men through Christ be actually present and attained "in the history of humanity."

We remain free to reject what has been revealed, of course. One thing that God never impinges on in His dealings with us is our freedom even to reject Him. The individual and frequent exercise of this freedom to reject explains, I suspect, the length of time between the Ascension and the end of all things as we know them.

The Holy Spirit is concerned with countering the effects of such free sins.

> "Sin" means the incredulity that Jesus encountered among "His own," beginning with the people of His own town, Nazareth. Sin means the rejection of His mission, a rejection that will cause people to condemn Him to death.[49]

In his sermon for Pentecost, 2010, Benedict explained that "the Church never remains a prisoner within political, racial, and cultural confines; she cannot be confused with States nor with Federations of States, because her unity is of a different type and aspires to transcend every human frontier." The unity of the Church is the work of the Holy Spirit, who assures us that our

---

[48] John Paul II, *Dominum et Vivificantem* (May 18, 1986), no. 5.
[49] Ibid., no. 27.

ultimate end is not political. It transcends each of us, no matter what political regime we live in.

"Jesus always lives His intercessional priesthood," Benedict explains, "on behalf of the people of God and humanity and so prays for all of us, asking the Father for the gift of the Holy Spirit." We exist to reach eternal life, again if we choose it. We do so in the context of the lives we lead, surrounded, as we are, by those, too, who are called to eternal life.

Chapter 39

⌒

Pentecost: The Great Christian Teaching[50]

*Where men situate themselves in the place of God,
they can only find themselves struggling one against the
other. Where, on the other hand, they place themselves
in the truth of the Lord, they open themselves to the action of His Spirit which sustains and unifies them.*

—Pope Benedict XVI, Homily, May 27, 2012

This year, the Pentecost Mass in St. Peter's was accompanied by
the choir of the Academy of Saint Cecelia and its youth orches-
tra. The Holy Father broached one of the most difficult of all
Christian teachings: How is it possible, as we are commanded,
to love everyone, whereas we have neither the time, nor the
opportunity, nor even the desire to do so? The pope wants us to
reflect on an aspect of Pentecost that remains true.

Pentecost is the feast of the union of the Church, of the
communion of all humanity with one another. Aristotle had
insisted that the more friends we have, the fewer good friends we
have. Yet Christianity comes along, without necessarily denying

[50] Published in *Catholic World Report*, May 29, 2012.

Aristotle's point, to tell us that we should go out to everyone. We are also warned about friends who can corrupt us. We have to choose carefully. Plato's idea of friends being friends with everyone needs careful distinctions, as Aristotle also said.

Benedict points out how modern means of communication seem to bring us closer together no matter where we are in the world. Yet people choose to remain in their own "I." Is there a place for a genuine "we"? We can learn something from the Old Testament story of the Tower of Babel, which account seems directly implied when, on Pentecost morning, the Apostles, through the gift the Holy Spirit, began to speak in different tongues. Benedict recalls that the men at the time of Babel wanted to challenge God with a tower that would do what only God could do. To do this construction, they needed to communicate with each other.

God's response to this defiance was to give them all different languages so they could not understand each other. Obviously, the diversity of languages still seems both a curse and a blessing. It seems that all men should be able to understand each other. Yet the diversity of languages is a thing of beauty and allows us to live in smaller groups. The pope tells us that Pentecost is the "feast of the union, comprehension, and communion of all men."

We human beings have a common origin and destiny even when we do not understand each other's language. Yet it seems that the more we can communicate across the world in a few seconds, the less we understand about each other. People prefer to remain isolated in themselves. The essential element of a human being, however, is the capacity "to agree, to understand, and to act together." We cannot be content with simple otherness that denies a common nature and origin.

Pentecost: The Great Christian Teaching

* * *

This biblical story of the tower refers to a constant truth that recurs "throughout history." With the progress of science and technology, we realize that we can "dominate the forces of nature. We can manipulate the elements. We can fabricate living beings that are somehow joined with human beings." If we can do such extraordinary things, why do we need "to pray to God"? Benedict rhetorically asks. "We can construct any city that we want." Yet, we fail to see that we are, in fact, simply "repeating" the account of Babel. We have made many devices whereby we can transmit words and sights. Yet have we increased or decreased out capacity to "understand" one another?

And so "can we truly be united, at concord? If so, how?" The scriptural answer to this question is the "gifts of the Holy Spirit." What keeps us apart or unites us are not primarily tools and techniques. We need a new heart and tongue. It has to do with what we believe and love. We need the "fire" of the Holy Spirit so that we can be "transformed."

"What kind of an answer is this?" we wonder. The pope takes the solutions to our human problems out of our own hands, where we insist that they belong. At Pentecost itself, it was the Spirit that allowed the Apostles to speak in many tongues to announce the good news that Christ had died and risen. The inability of mankind to communicate is not a technical problem. It is a problem of the soul and of what man is.

Benedict next turns to John 16:13: "When the Spirit of truth comes, he will guide you into all the truth." Jesus says that the Church is the "place" where this truth is found. Our unity and disunity have to do with what we believe. When we speak as Christians, we do not speak just our own words from within our own "I." This priority remains true today. "The whole truth is

Jesus." The deeper disunity of mankind has to do with how they stand to this truth.

The fact that Jesus is the Son of God is what the Holy Spirit witnesses to. The Spirit guides us to a deeper knowing and understanding of Jesus. We become capable of knowing and understanding others only in the "we" of the Church. We need a profound humility to know what we are. It becomes clear, then, why Babel is Babel and Pentecost is Pentecost. "When men wish to make themselves to be God, they can only set themselves one against the other." Where they have the truth of the Lord, they open themselves to the "action" of the Holy Spirit. What goes on in the nations is not only international relations, which is, perhaps, why international relations do not understand the world.

To explain this difference between the spirit of Babel and that of Pentecost, Benedict cites Paul, who tells us to "walk by the Spirit" (Gal. 5:16). Paul explains to us that our interior lives are full of interior conflicts, of division. These are the works of the "flesh," as Paul calls the effects of sin. It is not possible that we be both "egoists and generous; we cannot dominate others and have the joy of serving them disinterestedly."

* * *

The pope notices also that Paul says that the self is full of covetousness, immorality, discords, jealousies, and dissensions. These are not Christian actions. If we live in the Spirit, we experience joy, love, and peace. The Apostle used the plural when describing disorders of the soul but a singular word when referring to each gift of the Holy Spirit. We need to pray that we follow the "Spirit of Truth."

This truth is transmitted to us in the Church. As Christ ascended to Heaven, He asked the Apostles to be prepared to receive the "Spirit of Truth." This mission is still in the world and for the same reason. We should not be overly surprised at the nature and direction of mankind, whose first premise at world building is that it is exclusively in his own hands.

The mandate to love everyone is not intended to deny the reality of friendship in this life. It is rather to say with Paul that if we have the same Spirit, we can live in peace and concord with everyone. The more universal brotherhood is something for eternal life, but it is prefigured at Pentecost in the charge that the Spirit sent by Christ gave to the Apostles.

The truths that the Apostles taught about who Jesus is can be the only real basis of human unity, even in this world. Mankind may strive to prove the opposite. In doing so, mankind will, like the builders of the Tower, find that they cannot reach God by their own methods.

God does not neglect us. We often just choose not to know what He did (and He definitely did not encourage us to build our own tower). The great Christian teaching began, as the Church did, on the Day of Pentecost, when Christ sent the "Spirit of Truth" to remain among us all days.

Chapter 40

~

The Trinity: The Ultimate Truth[51]

The Holy Father dedicated the millennial year 2000 to the Trinity. How do we grasp this theme? In my memory, I associate the Trinity with Frank Sheed, who wrote so well about it. I recall two addresses of Sheed that I heard: one at Catholic University in the 1950s and the other at the University of San Francisco in the late '60s or early '70s.

In one of these lectures, Sheed, a most amusing man, recalled his public speaking at London's Hyde Park Corner. There, he said, he talked about practically everything. But, he told us with some earnestness, he was struck by the fact that whenever he talked about the Trinity, no matter what the audience — atheist to Catholic — a certain hush fell on the crowd, followed by a careful listening not experienced with other theological or philosophical topics.

The central chapter of the first book I wrote, *Redeeming the Time*, was entitled "The Trinity: God Is Not Alone." This chapter, of course, responded precisely to an opinion expressed in Aristotle: his philosophical concern that God was perhaps "lonely,"

[51] Published in *Crisis Magazine*, 2000.

that He had no friends. Aristotle had taken thought about as far as it could go. Somehow it seemed to lead to a dead end, to an absurdity. God did not have what seemed most exalted in human experience. It took revelation to answer this loneliness problem.

God is Trinity.

In an instruction, the Abbot Columban asked, "Who, then, is God?" He answered: "He is Father, Son, and Holy Spirit, one God." Every word in that question and response is worth a book. God is a "who," evidently personal, not an "it." He is a "one." At the same time this "oneness" consists of "Father," "Son," and "Holy Spirit." Each of these words is carefully crafted, not arbitrary, not replaceable. Something irreducibly important is being said.

Columban goes on, "Do not look for any further answer concerning God." "Why not?" we wonder. Aren't we supposed to figure out every intellectual enigma? Surely this doctrine of three and one is a puzzlement.

Columban is not entirely true to his word. He suggests a way to consider God. "Those who want to understand the unfathomable depths of God must first consider the world of nature. Knowledge of the Trinity is rightly compared to the depths of the sea." We cannot fathom those depths.

Thus, "the Godhead of the Trinity is found to be beyond the grasp of human understanding."

So, we are to consider the world of nature, where we evidently find some things we cannot understand, fathom. A pari, we have an even greater problem in understanding the Trinity.

This comparison reminds me of the class I teach on Augustine. (His *De Trinitate* is still the classic discussion of the Trinity.) On the first day of the classes devoted to *The Confessions*, I bring with me the Folio Society of London's "full elephant-hide" edition of *The Confessions*. Scott Walter gave it to me for Christmas in 1995. The frontispiece contains a colored print, from the Golden Legend Collection of saints. The reprint is of the famous, no doubt apocryphal, scene of Augustine, in episcopal miter and cope, standing by the side of a lake.

In the distance are the green hills and mansions of the City of God. On the other side of an inlet sits a little child busy counting the grains of sand on the shore. When Augustine, on inquiry, tells him that he cannot do that, the child responds, "Then neither can you fathom the depths of the subject you are thinking about." Of course, Augustine, walking along, had been thinking of precisely the Trinity.

Columban's last bit of advice was that "if anyone wants to know what he should believe, he must not imagine that he understands better through speech than through belief." More is found in that sentence than meets the eye. Plato had warned us not to seek the true "Republic" anywhere but in "speech." Augustine had taken up this line of thought. The true location of the "City of God" is not simply in "speech." It exists in the Trinity, to which we are each ordered.

The "hush" that Frank Sheed experienced in a crowd in which the Trinity is addressed should not surprise us. This is the *ultimate truth*, to which our every act and question tend. What is particularly "quieting" about "speech" about the Trinity, I think, is the revelation that God is not alone. The Godhead of the Trinity is happily "beyond," but not opposed to, human understanding. God is not wholly unintelligible to our finite minds. But we are not gods. This is why our minds are so alert when we hear of the Trinity. We do want to know, yes, to see "face-to-face."

Chapter 41

⌒

Corpus Christi[52]

The Vatican still celebrates the feast of the Body of Christ on the day it is supposed to be held, namely, the Thursday after Trinity Sunday. Pope Benedict XVI in his sermon in St. Peter's took occasion to correct a tendency since Vatican II to concentrate on the Mass itself while it is being celebrated, but to downplay the presence and holiness of the abiding Eucharistic presence in the tabernacle.

Sometimes a one-sided interpretation restricts a broader understanding of the Sacrament. "The just emphasis placed on the celebration of the Eucharist can turn out to lessen adoration as an act of faith and prayer turned to the Lord Jesus really present in the Sacrament of the Altar," Benedict explained. This shift has serious consequences in the prayer life of the faithful. "To concentrate everything on Jesus in the Eucharist, at the moment of Holy Mass, risks undervaluing His presence in the rest of time and existential space." This overemphasis lessens our realization of Christ's presence among us in all times and places, in our

---

[52] Published in *Catholic World Report*, June 10, 2012.

homes and neighborhoods. "The Sacrament of the Charity of Christ ought to permeate all our daily lives."

In fact, "it is a mistake to oppose the celebration and adoration as if one were against the other." The truth is just the opposite. The celebration of the most Holy Sacrament includes the entire spiritual ambiance in which the community can truly and properly celebrate the Eucharist. The liturgical action can express its full understanding only in the broader background of worship and interior life.

The encounter with Jesus in the Holy Mass is activated truly and fully when the community recognizes that He, in the Sacrament, is still "present" in their own homes and hearts after the Mass is ended. He remains with us in His "discreet and silent presence." He enables us to offer our daily gifts to His Father. "At the moment of adoration at Mass," Benedict tells us, "we are all on our knees, all at the same level. The common priesthood and the ministerial priesthood find themselves around the Eucharistic Sacrifice. We have seen this adoration many times in this Basilica of St. Peter as in the Youth Masses in Cologne, London, Zagreb, and Madrid. It is quite clear that the time of vigil preparation for Mass prepares the hearts so that the actual celebration is more fruitful.

"To stand silently for some time before the Lord present in the Eucharist is one of the most authentic experiences of our being Church." It "accompanies" us as we sing, or listen to the Word, or go together to Communion. "Communion and contemplation cannot be separated. They go together." To communicate truly with another person, "I must know him, know how to stand in silence near him, listen to him, and look with love upon him. True love and true friendship always live in reciprocal regard, in intense silence, full of respect and veneration so that the encounter is lived profoundly in a personal and not superficial manner." If we lack this depth, the communication becomes superficial. Rather in true communion "prepared by prayer" we can speak confidently to the Lord.

* * *

What about the very sacrality, or holiness, of the Eucharist itself?

We have seen a certain weakening in the authentic message of Scripture. In the 1960s and '70s, the Christian understanding was influenced by a "certain secularization."

It is true that the essence remains not in rites or in ancient sacrifices but in "Christ Himself, in His person, in His life, and in the paschal mystery." Nonetheless, about this Christian "newness" we should not conclude that the holy no longer exists but that it has found its "completion in Jesus Christ." The divine love is incarnate, thanks to Christ. "Sacredness is purer and more intense and, as we see in the commandments, more demanding." Observance of ritual is not enough. We need the purification of heart that the involvement in life brings about.

The sacred has an "educational" function. Our loss of its sense inevitably impoverishes the culture, in particular the formation of a new generation. If, for instance, we say in the name of a secularizing faith that we no longer need sacred signs or images, "if we abolish public processions of Corpus Christi," the spiritual profile of Rome will change. Our personal awareness will be "weakened."

We can even imagine a mother and father who deprive their children of all religious symbols in the name of a secularized faith. In practice, they are leaving the public field free to many surrogate images present in the society. Other rites and signs appear that risk becoming "idols."

The Reason for the Seasons

"God our Father has not made such a humanity." He has sent His Son into the world not to abolish but to complete "the sacred." At the height of this mission, at the Last Supper, Jesus instituted the sacrament of His Body and Blood, "the memorial of His paschal sacrifice." By doing so, He put Himself in the place of "ancient rituals." He did it, not in the abstract, but in the midst of a rite. He commanded the Apostles to "perpetuate" it. This is the supreme sign of the true Sacred, *which is He Himself.* "With such faith, dear brothers and sisters, we celebrate today and every day the Eucharistic mystery. We adore it as the center of our lives and the heart of the world."

Benedict XVI, I think, gently reminds us of the whole context of our faith and ritual. He is aware of how easily things spiritual can be distorted, but he is even more aware of their awesomeness when they are rightly understood.

Part 4

Ordinary Time

Chapter 42

⌒

Mass and "the Holy"[53]

A man who has lived in many parts of the country wrote: "The Mass is becoming less and less about the Mass and more about the music, special prayers for individuals, and announcements. Our Mass is always the short form. Somehow we seem to have lost the sense of the 'Holy' that we once had at Mass." Benedict XVI's *Spirit of the Liturgy* echoes this concern about the Mass. The Mass has often become subordinate to other agenda. We are not first a "Christian community" whose "feelings" the Mass expresses. The Mass, because of what it is, causes the community that is gathered to worship God in the manner that God, not the community, has indicated.

The most "unsuccessful" additions to the current Mass are, it strikes me, the Psalm after the Epistle and the made-up prayers of the faithful, almost all of which are already in the Roman Canon especially. I cringe when I hear us pray for the pope or the faithful departed twice, once in the prayers of the faithful and repeated in the Canon. Do the people who compose the

<hr />

[53] Published in *The Catholic Thing*, September 10, 2010.

petitions ever pray the canon? And, of course, the so-called kiss of peace needed dropping long ago: wrong signal, wrong time.

People once joined the Catholic Church encouraged by a sense of holiness that was manifest in the music and demeanor of the congregation. In many places, children have a modified rite from adults. This is often true for college students in campus ministries in comparison with their home parish. You dress up to go to most Protestant services; we seem to dress down to attend Mass.

The translation of the Mass used for the past quarter of century downplays many noble and elevated things found in the Tridentine Rite or even in the Novus Ordo. The new translation that will go into effect in 2011 finally addresses this weakness, originally based on the premise that Catholics in general are a little slow. You cannot use too exalted a language with them. The older assumption was that Catholics were, in fact, rather bright and could learn things they did not already know. They could appreciate beauty when they saw or heard it. As I never tire of saying, Catholicism is an intellectual religion to its very core. Why obscure it?

The Mass is the Sacrifice of the New Law. Our music, announcements, and intentions are not to distract us from what is happening. But one Mass exists in the history of the world because the Sacrifice of Christ was the Sacrifice of the man-God to whom all times and places are present. The proper way to worship God is not of our making, but of God's making. "Unless you eat this bread and drink this cup you shall not have everlasting life in you." The Lord does not fiddle with us.

Downgrading things like silence in Church, the presence of the Blessed Sacrament at all times, genuflecting, and solemnity has made the environment of Mass seem rather like an ice cream social. Now I do know about the drums and dancing at African Masses as well as the lengthy solemnity of the Byzantine liturgies. All of these customs surrounding the awe of Mass had to be gradually learned and lived in actual parishes.

On the Word side of Mass, something also has been lost. We have no real room for doctrinal sermons. Valiant efforts have been made to convince us that homilies on the changing cycles of readings are all we need, without any real connection of one passage to another in a systematic way. But this emphasis has produced generations of doctrinal illiterates.

Schall has no easy answer for this, of course. The Mass is not the only place we can and should hear the doctrine of faith spelled out to us. But again, to be a Catholic is to belong to an intellectually challenging revelation whose own Scripture, as Benedict points out, uses Greek philosophy to explain itself more clearly.

With Mass being said at any time of day or night, moreover, it has tended to become the only way of praying. The pope is often present at Vespers or Benediction to remind us of a broader heritage that is available to us. The same might be said for novenas, retreats, and Rosaries. However, I heard recently of a school retreat at which it was decided not to have Mass at all! That, too, is the logical conclusion of elevating society over cult.

The basic point remains. The Mass is the presence of "the Holy" among us. In not knowing this, it gradually becomes a series of musical scores, announcements, and greetings and prayers for your friends and for sundry causes. Such things have their place, but if they are the focus, we grope for the "the Holy" elsewhere.

Briefly, the Mass is "the Holy."

Chapter 43

⁓

Reflections on Saying Mass[54]

Every time I am at a Mass on Sunday or a solemnity when, contrary to the rules, the Creed is omitted, I wonder "why?" The Creed is that part of the Mass wherein we, individually and as a congregation, affirm, out loud, what in essence we hold to be true about the Godhead. We need to hear, affirm, and think about this *Credo*, as it is called; the Church needs to hear it affirmed.

I asked a friend of mine about this omission of the Creed. He told me of a parishioner he knew who noticed the same thing. He asked his pastor about it. The pastor told him that it was omitted because the Creed was "divisive"!

Now, the life of Christ itself was divisive. This division is what happened when He dwelt amongst us. "Suppose ye that I am come to give peace on earth? I tell you, Nay; but rather division" (Luke 12:51, KJV). The Trinity, the subject matter of the Creed, is divisive. Jews and Muslims, among others, reject it. There is practically no point of what we believe or know that is not "divisive" to someone. The logic of this dubious principle—skip

54 Published in *Ignatius Insight*, February 2006.

what is "divisive"—is to believe and proclaim precisely nothing as the essence of our faith.

Is nothingness what satisfies empty minds?

Another friend told me that many of the younger priests he knew do not wear vestments at private Masses. I have even heard of Mass in swimsuits. There is no warrant for this shedding of proper liturgical garb, except perhaps in the failure of bishops and superiors to insist on the normal rules of the Church. Too much bother, I guess.

Not infrequently these days, I find petition prayers after the Creed to last longer than the Canon of the Mass itself. Seemingly interminable lists of things to pray for, not infrequently of dubious political or moral import, are read. Not seldom, petitions merely repeat what is already in the Canon, which itself is also in the vernacular.

What happens at the amazingly poorly named "kiss of peace" is too amusing to recount. Even though the Holy See recently decided to keep it in place, still no aspect of the current Mass is more inappropriately placed in the rite. It distracts us from what is going on at Communion at the very moment we ought not to be so distracted. I believe that at the Brompton Oratory in London it is placed elsewhere. In *The Spirit of the Liturgy*, Josef Cardinal Ratzinger praises the Church of Zaire for placing it before the Presentation of the Gifts. He adds that this placing "would be desirable for the whole Roman Rite, insofar as the sign of peace is something we want to retain" (170). That is, we may not want to retain it.

The kneeling, standing, sitting, bowing, and genuflecting aspects of Mass and Communion are up for grabs and cause all sorts of needless controversy. No two parishes or dioceses seem to be exactly the same or even think they should be. When we visit a new parish, we often have that bewildered look about what is going to happen next. The old suspicions seem borne out in practice, that if you change one thing, on the grounds that it could be "otherwise," then everything connected with it will be changed. I sometimes wonder whether every parish will not end up having its own Liturgy, sort of like the Reformation.

If there is anything clear in the later Eucharistic documents of John Paul II, the Roman and National Liturgical Commissions, and Benedict XVI, it is that each priest should say Mass every day, even if he has to do so alone, and, unless ill or infirm, properly vested.

What is even clearer is that, granted cultural variety, the Liturgy is not up for grabs so that we can refashion it to suit our tastes in either doctrine, wording, or movement. It is not the private property of priest or bishop. On May 13, 2005, Benedict XVI said to the Roman clergy assembled in St. John Lateran, "We are not sent to proclaim ourselves or our personal opinions, but the mystery of Christ and, in Him, the measure of true humanism."

This admonition, which is really a kind of charter of freedom from the reigning mood of recurrent adaptation, is no doubt aimed at "actor priests." Josef Ratzinger has often remarked that today the priest must, like John the Baptist, "decrease." The show is not about him. He is not there to call attention to himself, expound his own ideas, or entertain the people, a temptation almost endemic, as Ratzinger also indicates, to "turning the altar around."

The Mass is not a staged drama at which we applaud the talent of the performers. There really is room for quiet and awe. The priest is there to do what the Church asks in the way the Church asks it. Both of these criteria are set down in official documents and are easy to understand by almost anyone who takes the trouble to read them.

For a long time, following publication of the *General Catechism* and the *Code of Canon Law*, I have thought that what the Vatican especially needs to do is to establish a universal popular Missal, an *editio typica*, on which all others everywhere in the Church would be based. We need to get rid of the leaflet missals, burn them all as Luther, I believe, is said to have wanted to do to the works of Aristotle.

Each person in every parish should have his own Missal, which should not be changed every month, or year. The same Missal that we take to Mass at twenty should still be used at seventy. It is a great comfort to die with the same Missal we have used all our lives. I do recognize that many of the current English translations, especially of the Collects, range from atrocious to vapid in comparison with the Latin originals.

Each language group should have a common Missal, easily purchased in expensive or inexpensive versions. On one side would be the official Latin text, the same in all missals; on the opposite page the corresponding vernacular—whether German, Greek, Arabic, English, French, Spanish, whatever—in exact translation. Nothing is wrong with old, familiar translations. The rubrics about what the priest should do and wear should be quite clear in the text and easily known by the reader. Latin should be used once in a while, if not often. The translation is right there. Everyone has what is being said or sung right there in front of him.

I know there are theories that want to take away any reading or prayer tools (e.g., Rosaries and Missals) from the faithful so that they are completely beholden to whatever the celebrant (I dislike that word) comes up with. The Mass is absorbing, but only when it is what it is supposed to be. If I have to worry about whether it is orthodox or proper, I cannot follow it with attention. With no authentic text before them, people do not know what is supposed to happen. Today the Missal should be seen both as a prayer book, which it is, and as instruction and information about what is supposed to happen.

The laity have a right (it's in canon law), and should avail themselves of the duty, to inform bishops, and the Holy See, when what is laid down is not observed. How can they do this if they do not authentically know what is supposed to be going on? They should know that the clergy are bound to the same rules that they are reading about in the Missal. It is also their Mass in the sense that neither the clergy nor the laity themselves are permitted to make it up by themselves, but both must observe the same rite.

Even the slightest changes in wording and gesture usually imply a veering in thinking or understanding, even in doctrine. C. S. Lewis pointed out that we cannot say liturgical prayers together if the celebrant or other minister is making up the words as he goes along. The Mass words are very precise, very much expressive of a definite, well thought out, defined understanding of who the Father is, who Christ is, and what this sacrifice of the Mass is about in each of its details.

Moreover, there is absolutely nothing wrong with reading what is also being said. In fact, it is often a help in praying the Mass, both because rarely in the average church are the acoustics and pronunciations clear enough for everyone to hear and because understanding takes constant repetition and attention.

"The Pope is not an absolute monarch whose thoughts and desires are law," Benedict XVI remarked at a Mass on May 7, 2005, also in St. John Lateran. "On the contrary: the Pope's ministry is a guarantee of obedience to Christ and to His Word. He must not proclaim his own ideas, but rather constantly bind himself and the Church to obedience to God's Word, in the face of every attempt to adapt it or water it down, and every form of opportunism."

This spirit, of course, is what we should follow with regard to the Mass. We are a literate and intelligent people. Our Faith is also directed to intellect. We should not only know what the Mass is supposed to be (because we too can read what it is intended to be); we should also encounter what it is when we attend it.

"The authority of the Pope is not unlimited," Josef Ratzinger wrote in *The Spirit of the Liturgy*. "It is at the service of Sacred Tradition. Still less is any kind of general 'freedom' of manufacture, degenerating into spontaneous improvisation, compatible with the essence of faith and liturgy. The greatness of the liturgy depends—we shall have to repeat this frequently—on its un-spontaneity" (166).

That is a worthy conclusion to what I want to say here: "the greatness of the liturgy depends on its un-spontaneity." It is unfortunate that we have to repeat this reminder so frequently.

Chapter 44

⁀

The Fourth Canon of the Mass[55]

Yet, you, who alone are good, the source of life, have made
all that is, so that you might fill your creatures with blessings
and bring joy to many of them by the glory of your light.

—*Roman Missal*, Preface to the Fourth Canon

Msgr. Robert Sokolowski, at Catholic University, commented to me that he had begun to use the Fourth Canon. The new translation was excellent. I seldom used this canon. It is used only with its proper Preface. So, I began to use it. Sometimes called the "Intellectual Canon," its origins are in St. Basil and the Eastern Liturgy. It needs listening to. And it pays to listen to it. It is a remarkably concise statement of the Faith, how it all fits together.

Canons are cast in the mode of praise and worship of the Father. They depict by name who is there "present" at any Mass. It is a surprising reality if we pay attention. Christ is there; that is what it is all about. Through Him we can worship and praise the Father in the first place, always in the Holy Spirit. We are

---

[55] Published in *The Catholic Thing*, 2013.

not there looking at ourselves. We all look to the Father of our Lord.

The angels and saints are named in various combinations in the four main canons. The pope and the local bishop are specifically identified. Our loved ones are recalled, also the dead, and those kneeling before the altar. The Blessed Mother is "venerated," not adored. St. Joseph, the Apostles, the early popes, and martyrs are listed. In short, the whole of creation is understood to be there.

We are not alone at Mass.

We are there as members of the Mystical Body of Christ. We are together, yet each of us directs himself to the Father through the Son and the Spirit. We are there because we are made for eternal life. But it is not achieved apart from our choice.

In the Preface, we state that what we do is "right and just."

To do what?

To give the Father "glory."

He existed before and will abide "for all ages." All goodness comes from the Father. He has made "all that is." The Father is the "light." He is the source of intelligence made manifest in the Word. And it is we who speak God's name "in exaltation." Significantly, the rest of creation receives its "voice" through us men. This giving voice, intelligence, to creatures, including ourselves, is part of why we exist.

The first part of the Fourth Canon is what I will consider here. It is rather long, certainly compared with the brief Second Canon. We first explain why we give "praise" to the Father. All His works are "fashioned in wisdom and love," including ourselves. (The intellectual efforts of human philosophy are to see and to explain that the world itself bears signs of intelligence, not simply of chaos.)

What about man himself?

He is made in God's "image." The whole of creation is "entrusted" to his care. He is to "have dominion over all creatures." What about the smallness of man and the enormity of the universe — the dark energy and the Higgs boson? Man is the one being from within the universe that reflectively looks at it. His responsibility is to know it, to know its order.

Next, we are brought up short. We are reminded that, in human history, we lost the initial divine "friendship" by "disobedience." This implies that the Creator is more interested in man than He is in the universe's gyrations.

But how does the Father respond to this "disobedience"?

Each man was created to reach eternal life. But God could not and did not want to force Himself on anyone. Each person had to choose God because He loved Him. So death was not the final word. God sent many messengers. He made many covenants to work out man's salvation.

Finally, God sent His own Son, born of the Virgin Mary. He was true God and true man, body and soul, like us in "all things but sin."

What did this Son do?

He told everybody, even the poor, the imprisoned, and the sorrowful — not only the wealthy and intelligent, but them, too — of their salvation, of what they really exist for and how to attain it.

How did He do this?

Through His death and rising again. We are thus no longer to live only for ourselves.

How could this be?

He sent the Holy Spirit from the Father.

Why?

The Reason for the Seasons

To "perfect" His initial work to "sanctify creation to the full." Such was the Father's "plan." This is what we see being worked out before us. It does make sense. We affirm that we understand that it does. Our "seeing" is the first step in praising the Father.

Part 5

From All Saints to the
Immaculate Conception

Chapter 45

⌒

All Saints' Day[56]

I seldom think of All Saints' Day without recalling Belloc's walk in 1902, recounted in *The Four Men*. The walk took place in his native Sussex County from October 29 until All Souls' Day. It is about our home and our heavenly home, so intimately related.

Each of the "four men" is Belloc.

On All Saints' Day, the "Poet," in a timely theme in the context of the failures of universities and ideologies, says: "For men become companionable by working with their bodies and not with their weary noodles, and the spinning out of stuff from oneself is an inhuman thing." I quite love that passage. The spinning out of theories as if *what is* did not exist is the greatest of the sins.

* * *

In Old English, this is All Hallows' Day. 'Tis a better name, I think. The "hallowed" we hold in awe. We do not do the hallowing; the Lord does. We think of the eve of All Hallows' Day. This eve disturbingly reminds us of those who are not saints, even of the damned.

[56] Published in *The Catholic Thing*, November 3, 2009.

The Reason for the Seasons

Leon Bloy said that the only sadness was not to be a saint.

But in this regard, Belloc's "Sailor" was right when he said to the "Poet and Myself: 'Let us go hence, my children and drink in the bar with common men, for the Devil will very soon come in by the window and fly away with these philosophers.'" The Devil, evidently, knows that they are the easier prey, and the ones that do the most damage when they go wrong.

That the Lord came also to save common men is what the feast of All Hallows is about. John Paul II evidently canonized more saints than all the rest of the popes put together. He had a livelier appreciation than most of those who work with their hands and not their noodles. When the Devil flew out of the bar, he did not take the common men, nor "Myself" (Belloc) nestling among them drinking his Audit Ale. The Devil only took the philosophers, who, evidently, also occasionally inhabit the pubs of Sussex County, though they are more comfortable in the universities to which the Devil has little need to fly.

Belloc records that on his walk "the air was clear and cold as befitted All Hallows' Day." The four men find an inn later in the day and are ushered into a dining room in which "some fifteen or twenty men, all hearty, some of them old, were assembled, and all were drinking and singing."

These men finished their meal. "We ordered ours, which was of such excellence in the way of eggs and bacon, as we had none of us until that moment thought possible upon this side of the grave." Lest the reader doubt, Schall is recalling these earthy deeds of an All Hallows' Day because they prefigure the Resurrection. That is the point: it includes our bodies and hence our companionship.

"The cheese also ... was put before us, and the new cottage loaves, so that this feast, unlike any other feast that yet was since the beginning of the world, exactly answered to all that the heart had expected of it, and we were contented and were filled." This eating and drinking is the very opposite of materialism. It defies it, in fact, by showing us the souls of men in bodies that together are hallowed.

The four men light their pipes. They call for drinks. Myself drinks black-currant port. Grizzlebeard drinks brandy. The Poet has beer and the Sailor drinks claret. "Then, these before us, we sat ourselves at the great table, and saluted the company." This is the "worldliness" that is Christian, the one that is happily content that the Word did indeed become flesh to dwell amongst us.

Chapter 46

⁓

On Saints and Souls[57]

The modern world has a peculiar problem with Catholicism. Few acknowledge that such a thing as "sin" exists. But an occult delight surges in many souls over the frequent aberrations of believers. A twofold reason exists for this reaction. First, the track record of believers is consolingly not much different from that of unbelievers. Secondly, no need to distinguish right from wrong, good from bad, can be given if no one can do anything about them. Yet we recollect the nagging teaching that Christ became man, in part, so that sins might be forgiven. The denial that sins happen logically denies the need or reality of a forgiving God.

In the Church, the first two days of November are the feasts of All Saints and All Souls. Pope Benedict often gave, as evidence for the validity of Catholicism, the example of the saints, from all walks of life. Morality is not primarily a list of rules or series of sanctions. It is mainly the following the example of those who loved God and neighbor, who served the minds and bodies of their friends and fellow men.

---

[57] Published in *The Catholic Thing*, November 1, 2013.

The Reason for the Seasons

Prominent in the list of actual saints are those known to have been, by any objective standards, sinners. This approach teaches us that sin itself need be not the last word, though it can be, if we choose. Sin is the other side of human freedom. To deny the possibility and fact of sin is to deny the possibility and fact of human freedom.

Benedict has likewise devoted much attention to the souls of the departed. The teaching on souls in Purgatory has recently been downgraded, if not simply rejected. Yet it is the primary doctrine that stands, as it were, between saints and sinners. All Saints' Day is a celebration of all the saints who have ever reached the purpose of their lives, the City of God, the achievement of the end for which each person is created.

All Souls' Day refers rather to the probably far larger number of people who died repentant indeed but not yet really ready to encounter the divine life. Benedict, along with Plato on the same topic, suggests that no one would want to stand before God unless he was sufficiently cleansed. He leaves the logic to sink in.

We hear of the Church Suffering, the Church Militant, and the Church Triumphant. The same Church is understood to have members in Heaven, in Purgatory, and still deciding on where they will be. Obviously, left out are those who have simply and responsibly rejected entrance into such Church at any level. The last section of Hobbes's *Leviathan* was entitled "The Kingdom of Darkness."

Benedict devotes much attention to the following phrase in the Creed: "Christ will come to judge the living and the dead." Why is this? Readers of Plato — Benedict is one of these — know that Socrates was concerned to show that the world was not created in injustice. Man was not "the measure of all things," as Protagoras had suggested. If he were, nothing we do would make much difference. This consequence would mean that crimes and sins that men committed in this life were not accounted for if they were not repented or punished. It would also mean that the many noble and good, but unacknowledged, things that we do for one another would not be recognized.

The doctrine of Hell, if nothing else, testifies to the significance of our actual deeds, however we might judge them in our own interest. Plato understood this issue quite clearly. In Plato, if we die in our sins, we are condemned to the river of punishment. We cannot escape until the person against whom we sinned forgives us.

What Christianity adds to this teaching on forgiveness is that our sins are not simply against one another; or better, as they are against one another, they are also against God, who placed us in the order in which we live, the order of our freedom and responsibility. Christian revelation begins its teaching to us with the word "Repent." This admonition implies that we have the graced power to do so. But we do not have the power to forgive ourselves, since it is not only against ourselves that we have sinned.

How often shall we forgive our neighbor? Christ answered this question of the Apostle by saying not just seven times, but seventy times seven times. That is to say, the core of our issues with God remains as long as we have our freedom. But we can choose either way. This choosing is what we do in the drama of our lives. All Saints and All Souls—these two days, if we think of them, reach the very foundations of our being.

Chapter 47

≈

All Souls' Day: "The Day of the Dead"[58]

One of the most beautiful Masses of the Liturgical Year is that of All Saints' Day, on November 1. I have always loved this Mass. Its first reading is that from Revelation about the Great Gathering; the second is from John's Epistle about our seeing God as He really is, a doctrine whose only fault is that it is, as Chesterton said, too good to be true. Finally, the Gospel is from Matthew about our being glad that our reward is great in Heaven.

We often forget the sheer beauty of the Masses we hear. Even more, we forget that our religion is unique in that it promises the highest things precisely to *us*, not to some abstraction or grouping down the eons of time. Christianity is not a selfish religion, but it is a religion that forbids us to doubt that we shall see God, unless, of course, we choose not to see Him. Such is our liberty.

The day following All Saints' Day is All Souls' Day. Traditionally, the Church dedicates the whole month of November to prayers for the souls in Purgatory. All Souls is the day on which we remember the dead, our dead. Christianity is not, strictly speaking, a "soul" philosophy or religion. We love Plato, but we

[58] Published in *Crisis Magazine*, November 1992.

are not Platonists. The immortality of the soul is not originally a Christian doctrine but a Greek philosophical conclusion, no less valid for all that.

All Souls' Day, furthermore, is not about the Greek philosophical doctrine, which is most useful in Christianity, but about those of our dead who are not yet with God. In recent times there has been something of a shadow cast on All Souls' Day by the way Masses for the Dead are celebrated, as if all the trappings of Heaven are immediately and definitely acquired at any death.

But Christianity at its best takes the power of evil much more seriously than a kind of automatic resolving of our problems and the dubious record of our deeds at death. Christianity—perhaps I should say Catholicism—thinks that the power of choice is so fundamental, so dangerous, if you will, that it somehow can reach beyond death. Those who would take away Purgatory and All Souls are those who would make the power of our choice to be flabby and inconsequential.

We have, to be sure, Memorial Day in May, a secular day in this country, having I believe rather much to do with our wars, especially World War I and Flanders Fields. In Catholic Europe, on the other hand, All Souls' Day is the day to visit the graves of our ancestors, our parents, family, and friends. It is a day in which to remember the tremendous doctrine of our freedom as it existed in the lives of those we loved.

All Souls' Day is a day of *remembering*—one of the great words of our metaphysics. It is a day of doctrine, of the realization of our ultimate dignity, that of creatures, free creatures, who have the power to reject God because they have the power to choose Him. I cannot, I confess, tolerate the wishy-washiness of those who save everyone at the cost of reducing all of our actions to insignificance, because, it is implied, there is nothing that we can do to offend God, whose essence is said to be a kind of universal "compassion" that does not care what we do or what we think, for that matter. No God who gave us the Commandments thinks this way.

In the Breviary for All Souls' Day, there is a wonderful passage from a book that St. Ambrose of Milan wrote on the death of his brother Satyrus. I do not want to reflect on this whole passage. But I do want to cite the part in which Ambrose refers to immortality. He puts it in a way I had never seen before. "Death was not part of nature; it became part of nature," Ambrose wrote.

> God did not decree death from the beginning; He prescribed it as a remedy. Human life was condemned because of sin to unremitting labor and unbearable sorrow and so began to experience the burden of wretchedness. There had to be a limit to its evils; death had to restore what life had forfeited. Without the assistance of grace, immortality is more of a burden than a blessing.

We sometimes forget, though Plato did not, that the philosophical doctrine of immortality does not by itself solve the problem of happiness.

To have an immortal soul, then, does not by itself decide how we live or choose through the souls that animate us. This is why both our blessings and our punishments, even unto a Hell, are more dramatic if we are in fact immortal. Ambrose was right; All Souls' Day was right. Without the doctrine of grace, the immortality of the soul is more a burden than a blessing.

We are said to live in a world that has no need of God. When we hear this sort of thing, we should not forget that this is a "proposition" not at all established or proved. In such a proposition of not needing, we end up with a world that has no "need" of much of anything because in order for something to be truly needed, it must somehow have a transcendent purpose about it, even if it be the most finite of finite things.

The immortality of the soul, as I said, is originally a Greek doctrine. It is a philosophical doctrine. This origin in reason does not mean that Christians do not hold it, do not think it necessary for their own faith. The only way that we can hold Christianity to be true is to hold that something that is not specifically Christian is true, that which is presupposed to anything being true at all. The central doctrine of Christianity about our destiny is not the immortality of the soul but the resurrection of the body, a much more consoling, and at the same time, much more defiant doctrine.

The immortality of the soul, however, is needed to account for the continuity between our lives and the resurrection of the body. Without the doctrine of the immortality of the soul, we cannot account for the fact that the person who actually died is the same one who shall rise again. This point is what the Christian doctrine is about in the first place. If we, as unique individuals with our own names, are utterly destroyed at death, but God "re-creates" us in the resurrection, then we are simply not "us." And to be ourselves is precisely what we want to be, even unto everlasting. This is something at least hinted at by Aristotle when he remarked that we do not want our friends to become something other than they are — gods, for example.

But if our souls are immortal, whether unto good or unto evil, as Plato suggested in book 10 of the *Republic*, then there must be some relation between them all, again for better or worse. All Souls' Day, if you will, has to do with the "for better" side of those who have died but whose lives were by no means completely honorable or holy in their lifetime choosings. There is nothing unchristian in saying that we need to be purified to see God. We would not want it otherwise.

How are we to understand this need, this "world" that includes souls of the living and the dead, the damned and the glorified? Some friends of mine happened to see recently the Folger Theatre production of Shakespeare's *Troilus and Cressida*, a play that I had never seen and may or may not have read. (I do not remember reading it, which says something not wholly complimentary about my education or my memory, or both.)

In any case, I happen to have the Viking *Complete Works of Shakespeare* (1977). In the introduction to *Troilus and Cressida*—a wonderful introduction, in my view—Professor Virgil K. Whitaker sets down a brief description of the "world" in which Shakespeare lived. In the context of All Souls' Day, I think it gives as good a description as any I have seen of "the world" that we presuppose in our tradition.

In this world of Shakespeare and his contemporaries, God was the Creator. He placed an order in nature at once hierarchical and universal. By being and doing what they were, the creatures that were not God "did their part in achieving His ultimate purposes." The order of things came about through the obedience of creatures to the physical, the moral, and the political laws.

This same human being, however, was free. He could choose not to obey these laws. Along with God and the angels, man possessed free will: each person possessed this power. To live rationally meant freely living according to the laws of God in all their manifestations. Man could also disobey them. This was his freedom. But his disobedience was not without its consequences in himself and others, even in some sense in the Deity itself, as the Incarnation suggests.

The Reason for the Seasons

The powers and appetites of men could cause them to break the laws they did not make. Such were the passions and emotions of men that their calm reason could be overshadowed, rejected, forgotten. But evil itself gives rise to suffering. We cannot but recall Tiresias's famous line in *Oedipus Rex*, "To be wise is to suffer." Nor can we forget Socrates's reminder that "it is better to suffer evil than to do it." Even with evil and suffering, we are not done with God.

Whitaker calls *Troilus and Cressida* Shakespeare's most "modern play." That is to say, we see the accounts of the evils we would do to one another without the overarching context of their understanding before God. What is such a world like?

> The modern reader does not need to be told that what passes for love is often lust, and that what motivates much patriotism has nothing to do with love of country. Modern literature has made these points in wearisome detail. But Shakespeare has intensified and clarified even this aspect of human nature.... His eye has roved from the councils of the mighty to the backbiting of their hangers-on. Modern fiction has done much better, moreover, at giving us a Cressida, or a Pandarus and Thersites, than at showing us a Hector betraying his intellect under the pressure of the moment or a Ulysses expending his wisdom on an intrigue to end a petty broil.... We may not like the people [in *Troilus and Cressida*], but they are with us everywhere. Shakespeare often tells us what we can be or should be. Here he tells us what, unfortunately, we all too often are. (978–979)

And if "this" is what we "all too often are," surely it is not so difficult to find a place for All Souls' Day, a day on which we

All Souls' Day: "The Day of the Dead"

realize that, although there are not a few saints among us, there are far more of what we can only call, following Shakespeare's logic and our own self-awareness, sinners.

As I did before (*Crisis*, November 1990), I cannot let this day pass without again recalling Belloc's *Four Men*, his walk through Sussex in 1902, a walk that ended on All Souls' Day. "I went till I suddenly remembered with the pang that catches men at the clang of bells what this time was in November," Belloc wrote.

> It was the day of the Dead. All that day I had so moved and thought alone and fasting, and now the light was failing. I had consumed the day in that deep wandering on the heights alone, and now it was evening. Just at that moment of memory I looked up and saw that I was there. I had come upon that lawn which I had fixed for all these hours to be my goal.

And in the end, that immortality that comes with memory of land, deed, family, and polity Belloc combined with the naming of things, with what we have done and not done, with the sorrow of our endings and the hope of our rising.

When Belloc left the oldest men of the four, who were indeed himself, Grizzlebeard said to the others:

> But I who am old will give you advice, which is this—to consider chiefly from now onward those *permanent things* which are, as it were, the shores of this age and the harbors of our glittering and pleasant but dangerous and wholly changeful sea.

> When he had said this (by which he meant Death), the other two, looking sadly at me, stood silent also for

about the time in which a man can say good-bye with reverence.

This is the world *that is*, isn't it? Shakespeare's world, Belloc's world, Sophocles' world, are where our lives seek the "harbors of our glittering and pleasant but dangerous and wholly change-ful sea."

Ambrose of Milan, to whom the young Augustine listened so carefully, wrote in the same discourse on the death of his brother: "Death is then no cause for mourning, something to be avoided, for the Son of God did not think it beneath His dignity, nor did He seek to escape it." In the passage from the book of Revelation on All Saints' Day, we read:

> And all the angels stood round the throne and round the elders and the four living creatures, and they fell on their faces before the throne and worshiped God, saying, "Amen! Blessing and glory and wisdom and thanksgiving and honor and power and might be to our God for ever and ever! Amen." (7:11–12)

We will understand modern man — understand what "unfor-tunately, we all too often are" — when we again know the rela-tion between All Saints' Day and All Souls' Day, when we again know with Plato the philosophical reasons for the immortality of our souls, but also with Ambrose, know why, "without the assistance of grace," this same "immortality is more of a burden than a blessing."

"To be wise is to suffer."

We said "good-bye with reverence" for "it was the Day of the Dead."

Chapter 48

All Souls and the "Permanent Things"[59]

A seminary in Ireland, now closed, was dedicated to the training of priests for foreign missions, for strange places such as California. It was called All Hallows — that is, All Saints, November 1.

Oxford University in England has a college called All Souls, which is November 2.

Taken together, all saints and all souls are designed to cover all of the final combinations of the human race except "all the still living" who are waiting to join one or the other of the previous categories. Come to think of it, all "all saints" have souls. What are left are "all lost souls," who, presumably, have already also made their final choices about how they are permanently to be.

Most of my relatives are buried in the Catholic cemetery just at the edge of Pocahontas, a small county seat in rural northwest Iowa. My mother's grandparents, my grandparents on both sides of my family, my mother herself, and, I believe, all but one of her thirteen brothers and sisters are buried in this neat cemetery. Two of my father's brothers are also there; his other brother is a few miles east in the cemetery in Clare. Two of my father's four

[59] Published in *Ignatius Insight*, November 2005.

sisters are buried there, plus numerous cousins and their families, though many are scattered in later years. My father is buried in the cemetery in Santa Clara, and my brother in the cemetery in Spokane.

On the second of November, many families, especially in small towns, decorate graves with flowers, have Masses or prayers said for their deceased relatives, and in general remember them. In modern cities, I think, we are in danger of losing contact with the dead in our families and in our culture. Families move. Cremation changes things. There are so many of us.

We do not have to be superstitious, of course. We believe in the immortality of the soul and the resurrection of the body. Our contact with cemeteries is designed to recall our very mortality but also to remind us of what we hold about death and its place in our lives.

As we get older, we find that many more members of our immediate family are dead than alive. We find friends gone. Such is our lot. To wish it otherwise, while not totally unhealthy an exercise, needs to be understood clearly. "It is appointed for men to die once, and after that comes judgment" (Heb. 9:27).

Death has become a hospital thing, not a home thing. The dead body is a source of "parts," to be somehow passed on to others. We think almost exclusively of the living, not of the dead.

We celebrate lives at funerals. We do not worry about souls and their fates. The elderly are a problem, even a social and political problem, not sources of wisdom. Cemeteries are often desired for the land they take up. Laws exist about how long cemeteries are to be kept intact. We notice that Latino and Oriental families somehow still take care of their own elderly at home, whereas with us this care is often passed on to various institutions, specialists. This may not be all bad, but we must reflect on it.

All Souls and the "Permanent Things"

* * *

Belloc's wonderful book *The Four Men* describes a walk he took in the English county of Sussex, from October 29 until All Souls' Day, 1902. As the four walkers reach the end of their walk, the old man, who, like the other three walkers, is Belloc himself, makes the following memorable farewell reflection:

> There is nothing at all that remains: not any house; nor any castle, however strong; nor any love, however tender and sound; not any comradeship among men, however hardy. Nothing remains but the things of which I will not speak, because we have spoken enough of them already during these four days. But I who am old will give you advice, which is this: to consider chiefly from now onward those permanent things which are, as it were, the shores of this age and the harbors of our glittering and pleasant but dangerous and wholly changeful sea.
>
> When he had said this (by which he meant Death), the other two, looking sadly at me, stood silent also for about the time in which a man can say good-bye with reverence. (57–58)

I have always been moved by this haunting passage, "nothing at all remains," "the glittering and pleasant but dangerous and wholly changeful sea," the "time in which a man can say good-bye with reverence."

In the Breviary, for the feast of All Souls, the Church includes a very powerful passage from St. Ambrose about the death of his brother Satyrus. This is a particularly significant reflection on death. Ambrose tells us that "Christ did not need to die if He did not want to." This position does not mean that Christ was a sort of suicide. It means that, as God, nothing could happen to

Him without His own will, which was itself in free obedience to the Father. Thus, the obvious question arises about why the Father might require this obedience.

To this question Ambrose adds that Christ "could have found no better means to save us than by dying." We can and do try to imagine a better way. We come up with alternatives. Much of ancient and modern thought is an attempt to find a suitable alternative to explain why the human condition is as it is. This same thought is quite disconcerted with the notion that the Christian explication might, after all, be true. The connection is between Christ's death and the saving of mankind. The former was necessary if the latter were to be accomplished, while protecting both divine and human liberty in the events leading to a proper salvation.

But why does mankind need saving? Why cannot it save itself? Ambrose continues: "Death was not part of nature; it became part of nature." This sentence must be examined. Clearly, it states that a finite being like man, the mortal, is naturally slated to die.

This view that death is not part of nature goes against all our thinking about what a finite creature like ourselves is. But such a mere mortal, born to die, never existed in fact.

From the beginning of God's intention in creation, the man who did exist was destined to a supernatural end, to participation in the inner life of God. This was something beyond what it is to be a human being as such. This possibility was due to something over and above what was naturally due to man. What we know as "original sin," that necessary but perplexing doctrine, is the reason the initial relation of man to his end did not come about. This Fall, as we call it, meant that death subsequently "became part of nature," in Ambrose's words.

We are all thus so interconnected that the actions of one person can affect all the others. If this connection with others were not possible, men would be naturally isolated from one another, not social animals. No one could stand such a solitary life. Ambrose continues, "God did not decree death from the beginning." "In the beginning," to use the first words of Genesis, God decreed no death for the particular man He in fact created and for his descendants. How did God "prescribe" death then? Ambrose says that He prescribed it in the actual context in which He found it — that is, in the context of Adam and Eve's choice, "as a remedy."

What a remarkable insight!

But a remedy? Death is a remedy?

What can this mean? How could precisely death "remedy anything"? Is this merely irony? It seems, in this context, that only "life" could be a remedy. But remember death is proposed as a remedy for what has happened as a result of the Fall, as a result of sin, all sin. Thus, something connected with the essence and nature of sin and its consequence justifies God in proposing the odd notion that "death" is a "remedy" for what has gone wrong in the human condition by man's own choosing.

* * *

Ambrose gives the following explanation of our fallen situation. He takes it to be based on something we all recognize. "Because of sin, human life was condemned to unremitting labor and unbearable sorrow and so began to experience the burden of wretchedness." These are almost the same words used in Genesis about what would happen to Adam and Eve if they ate of the Tree of the Knowledge of Good and Evil, that is, if they chose to make up their own laws.

The Reason for the Seasons

The origins of this wretchedness among us, about which wretchedness all the subsequent history of mankind attests, is not God. We are created good. We were offered a life with no death, but such a life had to be chosen. Otherwise, it would have been imposed on us. Hence, it would not really be ours. Without some "remedy" that we could not concoct for ourselves, this wretchedness would go on and on, even amidst our dying. Remember, the original purpose of God in creating us, that we be offered the inner life of God as our final destiny, never changed from the beginning.

The question now became: "How would this remedy work?" "There had to be a limit to its (wretchedness) evils." God is not defeated by evil, but He cannot act as if it did not happen. John Paul II maintained that what limits evil is "the Divine Mercy." That is, God allows evil to occur only insofar as He can, in spite of it, lead things back to His original purpose.

Ambrose then explains the terms of what must be done. "Death had to restore what life had forfeited." Again this is a thoroughly remarkable statement.

What had "life" forfeited?

Well, it forfeited the "not dying" that was originally offered as a gift over and beyond what human nature was in itself. It also forfeited thereby the original way that mankind was offered to participate in the inner life of the Godhead, which is, in itself, a life of infinite love that we describe as Trinity. No reason existed in God why He had to create anything in the first place. He had no deficiency or loneliness. Creation was in freedom, not necessity.

What, then, does death do?

That is, supposing no redemption, what will happen among our kind as a result of their own sinning and its consequences on others? "Without the assistance of grace, immortality is more of a burden than a blessing." What does Ambrose say here? First, he implies that we cannot redeem ourselves. We need a redeemer who is not just human, but still human. We need someone like unto us in all things "except sin," to recall Paul's words.

The soul, as the Greeks taught, is, however, itself naturally immortal. But that is an eerie kind of life from which also we need to be redeemed.

But why exactly would "immortality," which means, whatever its moral condition, the continuation forever of the soul without the body, be a "burden" and not a "blessing"?

First, we are not just souls and are not intended to be. Aristotle had already hinted at something of this point in his *tractate* on friendship, when he wondered if we would want our friend to be a god, that is, a pure spiritual being or soul? No, he thought, we want to be what we are: beings complete with bodies and souls. Thus, it would be "wretched" both to continue in a disordered life, even as a soul, and as an incomplete life without a body.

As we have already noted, the immortality of the soul is originally a Greek, not a Christian, teaching, though Christians also hold it to be true. The Christian use of the immortality of the soul is to explain how we are the same person who dies and who rises again. Without this connection provided by immortality, it is senseless to talk of personal continuity and even less of resurrection. What Ambrose says is that we need grace to accomplish this reunion. What we also need is someone who actually dies with the power to raise us up. And someone actually needs to atone for our sins. This is why Christ is central in any discussion of souls on All Souls' Day.

Our souls—or our minds as the active powers of our souls in knowing the order of things—do know "permanent things."

They know *what is*. And they know that they know. Socrates, at the end of his trial, figured that since his soul was immortal, he would continue to do what he always did, to speak and converse about the highest things with his friends. We do not disagree with this possibility. But we add that we also converse with God, become friends with God, not by our own power, but by grace through the death of Christ, which destroyed the death that was the punishment for sin.

Thus, All Saints' Day and All Souls' Day give us much to think about. On both days, we recognize that salvation includes keeping human beings as what they are even in redemption, or especially in redemption. On All Souls' Day we recall the dead; we realize that death is also given to us as a remedy. It is a remedy for our sins, for our lives in the midst of sins' consequences, for the wretchedness of lives and existence that would merely go on and on. The remedy is also a return to the initial purpose in creation. That is, we are still enabled, even in the midst of sin and death, freely to choose what we shall be. Not even God can make this latter choice for us. On this choice, and its implications, the real drama of the universe consists.

As Ambrose said, "Christ could have found no better way to save us than by dying." How long does it take to "say good-bye with reverence"? The real answer to this question is that we are not ultimately intended to say good-bye. This is why we were originally created without death. And this is why, when we are redeemed on the Cross, we are redeemed by One who says, succinctly, that "I no longer call you servants, but friends" (see John 15:15).

The friendship of man with God now includes death. But this death is now a remedy for, not the cause of, our wretchedness. Perhaps these are some of the things we can think about as we visit our cemeteries in early November, on All Hallows' Day and on All Souls' Day. When we walk in our cemeteries, we are reminded that, among the ultimately permanent things, we ourselves are included. Such is the meaning of these November days.

Chapter 49

＿

End Times: "The Secret Hidden from the Universe"[60]

The human being is not automatically well-ordered just because he sets his hope on natural well-being, even though it may be something as great as peace on earth and just order among nations. . . . Only the hope for God-given salvation, for eternal life, sets man right from within. . . . Not only does it renounce an activism totally enclosed within the plane of history and insistent that no hope is left when there is nothing more we can do; it also renounces the mere otherworldliness of a supernaturalism excluding history, which would abandon political humanity to fatalism.[61]

—Josef Pieper

More than one commentator has remarked on the spate of wars, rumors of war, earthquakes, floods, tornadoes, fires, terrorist bombings, tidal waves, and other such unpleasant happenings that we have recorded in recent months and years on this planet. The readings in the Liturgy for the last couple of weeks in the

---

[60] Published in *Ignatius Insight*, February 2005.

[61] *Josef Pieper: An Anthology* (San Francisco: Ignatius Press, 1989), 20–21.

The Reason for the Seasons

Liturgical Year and those at the beginning of Advent, moreover, recall, in one way or another, these same topics.

They also point to a solution, though not one we might expect. They speak of the "times and moments" known only to God, the warnings to be prepared, the knowing not the day or the hour.

Convulsions in the sun and the moon, floods, wars, earthquakes, plagues—all of these and more are mentioned or implied in Scripture for the End Times. The Church does not hesitate to have us read about them, always a sobering experience, whatever we are to make of them. They must be read carefully, of course. It is not uncommon in the history of Christianity to find folks waiting, so far prematurely, for the end of the world, based on a too literal reading of these passages.

The date of the so-called end of the world has been, indeed, quite a mobile one, and not something associated only with Jewish or Christian accounts. The books of Daniel and Revelation have been known to be read as a kind of events calendar with the main show scheduled for a certain date. When the event never comes to pass, doubt and ridicule are heaped on the whole business.

Still, these readings have been pondered for centuries, from the first moments in which they were uttered and recorded. Indeed, few subsequent decades in the past several thousand years have passed in which it was not possible to say, at the end of a given year, that at least some, if not all, of these rather unpleasant events happened around us somewhere in the world. Modern communications make every crisis seem as if it takes place in our backyard. We are as much concerned with crises in Virginia as in Japan, Hungary, Peru, or Pakistan.

We are still here, of course, though billions and billions of us have already passed in and out of our mortal life while the species man continues, even grows in numbers. There are considerably more of us now living and living longer and better lives on this green planet than ever before at one time. No matter how many of us have been eliminated by natural disasters, we go right on. Car accidents, abortion, cancer, and even crime are cumulatively much more lethal than natural disasters.

Nonetheless, we do not have to be professional astronomers to suspect that eventually the sun will cool, the planets will collapse, and life on this planet will be impossible, at least if we judge solely by what we know and can reasonably predict. Science fiction writers even want us to prepare for space travel so that at least some remnant of our kind will survive somewhere in the cosmos.

Evidently, such a catastrophic event is not in our immediate future, so we can relax. No doubt today, more people lie awake at night worried about the world supply of oil, itself a product of past eons, or the conditions of endangered bird species than those who worry about their immortal souls or the upcoming burned-out sun.

Apocalypses today, even natural disasters, are followed by efforts to find human culprits so that we can place praise or blame on those conceived to be the causes, or at least the causes of not being prepared or ready or effective. Sometimes it seems that we claim the right and power to prevent any cosmic event or local story from much bothering us.

The advocates of the big-bang and expanding-universe theories, however, have at least made us conscious that our time on earth, even as a species that comes and goes out of existence individually and sequentially, is, though generous, limited. Moreover, besides cosmic catastrophes that evidently will go on whether we like it or not, we have human catastrophes, which seem also to go on in some predictable manner. The November celebration of

The Reason for the Seasons

Veterans Day reminds us that human-caused disasters are often much more lethal than natural causes. Nothing in Scripture indicates to us that both sorts of problems will not go on as long as we remain on this earth, however much we seek "peace and justice."

We may reduce the incidence of such problems in a given time or place, but the same occurrences seem to rise up elsewhere or at another time. Our moral fiber is likewise as much challenged by natural as by human-caused disasters. Both cause enormous sufferings and call forth considerable sacrifices and virtue, so much so that one can almost wonder if there is not a plan to it all. Aquinas, after all, suggested that one of the reasons God allows evil, presumably both natural and human, is so that He can bring forth from its results virtues and good deeds that we would not see without them. Mercy is just one example.

* * *

Christianity holds that there is order in the universe and that we participate in that order after the manner of what we are, free and intelligent but finite beings whose personal destiny in each case is transcendent. That is, we are not just natural beings, but we are to participate in the inner life of the Trinity. We cannot get it out of our heads, moreover, that some relation between our moral order and the cosmic order does exist. Whatever we make of deterministic evolution theory, we do not think that it explains either itself or the obvious kinds of internal order we find in us, especially in living things. All this cosmic activity and variety is not going on just to be going on. Is not the very fact that we can wonder what is going on itself a hint that this wonder is not itself solely a product of determinism?

End Times: "The Secret Hidden from the Universe"

Scripture seems to speak of the End Times as occasioned not so much in terms of sidereal or planetary happenings as of human moral happenings. Their ominousness even seems to be a stimulus for more human metaphysical understanding of *what is*. Our relation to the world passes through our relation to one another and to God. This relationship is where the real drama of the universe exists; it is really why we are interested in it.

Cosmic things go on, to be sure, whether we are virtuous or viscous. Still, the just do not always triumph, nor even frequently. The unjust seem to rule over much of the land. We are perplexed that there is not a one-to-one relationship between rule and virtue. When Augustine entitled his famous book *The City of God*, he intended to teach us that this ultimate city we seek is not to be finally or directly found in this world.

Indeed, most scriptural descriptions of the End Times picture a rather foreboding scene. They indicate that mankind has gone too far in deviating from the measures or norms that are inbuilt in its mature members or in those advised by revelation. Men are pictured as too busy with other things to notice the signs of these events, which are intended to be warnings to them. The new heavens and new earth, which are also depicted, are not usually presented as alternatives to the more anxious descriptions but rather as what lies beyond them for those who are faithful. In other words, both forms of End Times are to work themselves out.

Too often, these depictions of the End Times are presented as if their primary purpose is to frighten us into being what we ought to be anyhow. Mankind is also warned that if it wills not to listen, not much can be done. Man's freedom will not be interfered with. I suspect, however, since it seems quite clear in Scripture itself that those to whom these descriptions and warnings seem to be addressed are not going to listen or much change their ways, they are rather intended to be presented as information about the way the world is, including the way human beings choose freely to form themselves.

The question of why there is a world at all, a cosmos, in which the sort of beings that we are can exist is one that deserves some reflection. Whatever we may think of the existence of other races of finite, intelligent beings elsewhere in the universe besides ourselves, the fact is that, even though they might be out there someplace, we do not know of them. Nor are they going to be substantially different from ourselves, though they may have chosen differently from us, as C. S. Lewis implied in his space trilogy and in Narnia. That is, they still will have to face the questions all intelligent beings face: Why do they exist rather than not exist? Why they are in the place they are? What can they know? What is their destiny? How they have been chosen?

They will be, in other words, finite, intelligent beings like ourselves looking out and realizing that they are the ones looking. Except by means of the intelligent beings within it, the universe itself sees nothing, as it has no organs of seeing or knowing.

In this sense, we are, on earth, probably in as good a place as any for questions of ultimate import to be asked. And they should be asked. It is perfectly all right to wonder what we are all about. It is also sensible to suspect that we are not merely the result of swirling deterministic accidents that randomly came up with ourselves asking why we randomly came up. That result—that even the random knowing is random and therefore not knowing—would, in fact, be much more startling than the notion that we are created by a God who does not, for His own being and happiness, need anything.

Still He had some purpose in mind in everything He caused to come forth out of nothingness, the imprint of which is found in everything that exists, including ourselves.

* * *

"The simplest truth about man is that he is a very strange being; almost in the sense of being a stranger on the earth," Chesterton wrote in *The Everlasting Man.*

> Alone among the animals, he is shaken with the beautiful madness called laughter; as if he had caught sight of some secret in the very shape of the universe hidden from the universe itself.... It is not natural to see man as a natural product. It is not common sense to call man a common object of the country or the seashore. It is not seeing straight to see him as an animal. It is not sane. It sins against the light; against that broad daylight of proportion which is the principle of all reality. (chap. 1)

The themes of Chesterton — that man is the real stranger on earth, that he remains homesick at home, that he is not a natural product of nature — are the ones that reflections on End Times constantly bring up.

We notice that in Chesterton a secret remains hidden from us. Our laughter, that great mystery of our everyday living, hints at the very "shape" of the universe that is otherwise hidden from us. The counterpoint to End Times is not nothingness, but times that do not end. Aquinas, commenting on Aristotle's notion of the eternity of the world, a world that repeated itself again and again, agreed with Aristotle that an eternal finite world was possible. He was not just speaking paradoxically but intended to be very precise. Aquinas meant that God as Creator might have created — though, as we know from revelation, did not in fact create—a finite universe that was kept in existence eternally, in the eternity of God. This did not make it either God or anything more than it was.

The conclusion we draw from this penetrating remark of Aquinas on Aristotle's equally penetrating insight? It is that this precise world in all its incredible particularity, a particularity that includes us in our particular history, in our particular era, in our particular planet, is the scene of a drama about man's relation to God, whence he came. The cosmos itself was created for a divine purpose that was not simply that of beholding the cosmos itself in its admittedly incredible glory.

Man, each man, is more important than the cosmos.

This is our dignity, in spite of the many theories that argue or imply that we have no dignity because the universe has no inner or external reason. Nor are even we ourselves created just to be beheld. We are created to act, to judge why we are and accept the fact that we are, even while remaining finite and rational beings, infinitely more than natural beings. "It is not natural to see man as a natural product," as Chesterton said.

We are not even well-ordered, as Pieper said, even when we fulfill noble, world-historic tasks. These may be included in what it is to love God by loving our neighbor, but this is not the reason each of us is created. And we cannot avoid the existence of our own being's transcendent purpose even when we deny it. That too is but another way of affirming that we have to choose what we are. The End Times, then, as they are presented to us, are designed to remind us of what we are—strangers in the universe—because the universe and its tasks, whatever they be, is not itself immediately the reason we exist.

There is only one drama in the universe, a drama that repeats itself in each human life that has ever existed. That is the drama

according to which he must freely decide whether the world and
with it himself have no meaning, or whether what he is given,
the "now without end," is the reason for his existence in the
first place. However posed, the decision is always free. There is
no other way in which the highest things could be given to us
and be ours.

*Only the hope for God-given salvation, for eternal life, sets man
right from within.* Indeed, a "secret of the universe" that is "hidden
from the universe itself" can be suspected.

Only that being who can see and know the universe from
within can suspect the laughter, the joy, the "mirth," as Chesterton called it in *Orthodoxy*, in which it was initially conceived
and made to be. Such are the things we learn from wondering
about why we are told so solemnly each year about End Times.

Chapter 50

⁀

Lord of the World[62]

In 2001 (surely not on 9/11!), St. Augustine's Press published a new edition of Robert Hugh Benson's 1907 novel, *Lord of the World*. A friend of mine in Vermont recently urged me to read it. I did.

Ralph McInerny, in a brief introduction, writes: "The novel wonderfully conveys the flatness and boredom of a world without God. Boredom becomes a condition for recognizing our need for something more than this—a few more decades of life and then a total void."

This novel is remarkably similar in theme to Pope Benedict's encyclical *Spe Salvi*, one of the very great encyclicals. That is, the novel is about the futility of a this-worldly utopia with the instruments of death (abortion, euthanasia) and endless death (prolongation of life, cloning) that are designed to make it come about. Indeed, in a lecture he gave at the Catholic University in Milan on February 6, 1992, Josef Ratzinger cited *Lord of the World* and the deadly Universalist, inner-world atmosphere it depicted.

---

[62] Published in *Inside Catholic*, March 9, 2009.

The Reason for the Seasons

My father had this Benson novel around the house when I was a boy in Iowa. I remember reading it. What, at a young age, I remember most about it was how frightening it was to me with its vivid end-of-the world description. Indeed, I have often said that this novel and C. S. Lewis's *That Hideous Strength* are the most frightening books that I have ever read. Now, no longer a youth, and then some, when I ask myself why this fright, it is because both books make the this-worldly triumph of evil so plausible, so intellectual, so logical.

Both books seem to exemplify the validity of a remark of Herbert Deane in his book on Augustine: "As history draws to its close, the number of true Christians in the world will decline rather than increase. His [Augustine's] words give no support to the hope that the world will gradually be brought to belief in Christ and that earthly society can be transformed, step by step, into the kingdom of God."[63] The anti-Christ figure in *Lord of the World* becomes the "Man-God," the "Lord of the World," precisely by promising universal brotherhood, peace, and love, but no transcendence.

The hero of the book is an English priest, Percy Franklin, who looks almost exactly like the mysterious Julian Felsenburgh, an American senator from, yes, Vermont. Felsenburgh suddenly appears as a lone and dramatic figure promising the world goodness if it but follow him. No one quite knows who he is or where he is from, but his voice mesmerizes. Under his leadership, East and West join. War is abolished. Felsenburgh becomes the president of Europe, then of the world, by popular acclaim. Everyone is fascinated with him. Still no one knows much about him. People

---

[63] Herbert Deane, *The Political and Social Ideas of St. Augustine* (New York: Columbia University Press, 1963), 38.

are both riveted and frightened by the way he demands attention. Most follow without question.

The only group who in any sense oppose him are the few loyal Catholics. The English priest is eventually called to Rome, since he has been an acute observer of the rise of Felsenburgh and his agenda. Apostasies among bishops and priests increase. The pope, John XXIV, is a good man, not unlike Pius X, who was pope when this novel was written.

Belief in God is to be replaced by belief in man. All those who oppose this doctrine are slated for extermination. With the English priest's inspiration, the pope forms a new religious order, the Order of Christ Crucified. Its members, including the pope, vow to die in the name of the Faith.

Many do.

The English prime minister and his wife are characters in a subplot. The wife desperately wants to believe in this new world movement. But she is horrified when she sees the killings that are justified in the name of world unity. The prime minister's mother, meantime, is brought back to the Faith by the English priest, much to the horror of the prime minister. But the wife is upset at the whole thing. Finally, to escape it all, she applies for and is granted public euthanasia. She dies not believing, but somehow knowing that what is coming with Felsenburgh is utterly horrible.

As the world comes to an end, the pope calls all the cardinals to Rome. Meantime, some English Catholics, against orders, plot to blow up the abbey where the politicians meet. Percy Franklin (now a cardinal) and a German cardinal are sent to England to try to prevent this plot, which they have been warned about. But word gets out. In retaliation, Felsenburgh orders that Rome be destroyed, which it is, together with the pope and all the

cardinals but the three not in Rome. These three quickly elect
the younger Englishman as the new pope, Sylvester III. The old
cardinal in Jerusalem dies. The German cardinal is hanged.

The last pope goes to the Holy Land, to the places of the
last days pictured in the New Testament. In a final act, Felsenburgh and all the world leaders fly in formation to destroy the
remaining signs of faith on earth. In response, Sylvester and the
remaining Catholics are at Mass. As they sing together the music of Benediction, the "Tantum Ergo," the attack strikes. With
that, the world ends.

The last words of the novel are: "Then this world passed, and
the glory of it." It could not be more dramatic, or more moving.
Somehow, I no longer find it so frightening. It is almost consoling.

Chapter 51

＞

"The World's Last Night"[64]

Provocative titles are meant to, well, provoke. I have always considered C. S. Lewis's little 1952 book of essays entitled *The World's Last Night* to be one difficult to forget. It takes its title from the last essay in the book, itself redolent of Christian apocalypse. Why does it provoke? Lewis was one of the few writers willing and able to address the question of "our last night" in this world both intelligently and seriously.

Clearly, the world's last end does not mean simply an accidental day in which the cycle of time just stops ticking. It means rather a moment in which all has been completed according to a plan that has been progressing since a beginning in time. It is a night (or day) in which everyone who ever lived on this planet will be involved through a judgment.

Other forms of apocalypse exist. Marxism was largely apocalyptic. Much of modern science, likewise, when it seeks to cure all evils and rectify all disorders, has more than a touch of it. The relation of "black" magic to "white" magic is not as distant in purpose as we sometimes like to think. I have just read an

---

[64] Published in *The University Bookman*, Fall 2014.

account of the goal of the new caliphate in the Islamic State. It
seeks to complete the true mission of Islam, which is to make the
whole world subject to Allah, to his unchanging Law, to which
all are converted or killed, where no places of exile or escape are
left, no monuments of alien belief or unbelief left standing. This
is, perhaps, a darker inner-worldly form of the world's last night.

The essay prior to the last one in the Lewis book is entitled
"Religion and Rocketry," itself rather a provocative title. These
essays obviously reflect Lewis's space trilogy—*Out of the Silent
Planet*, *Perelandra*, and *That Hideous Strength*—in which the dif-
fering eschatological statuses that we might conceive for man's
destiny are pictured in the form of the lives of races on other
planets. The earth is the "silent" planet in the universe because it
contains a fallen, but redeemed race of finite human beings. We
can conceive of a race that did not fall in the first place, or one
that fell and totally rejected any offer of subsequent redemption.

Near the end of the rocketry essay, we read: "Christians and
their opponents again and again expect that some new discovery
will either turn matters of faith into matters of knowledge, or else
reduce them to patent absurdities. But it has never happened.
What we believe always remains intellectually possible; it never
becomes intellectually compulsive." These words are carefully
chosen. All through the modern world, we have seen a series
of scientific inventions or philosophical/political theories that
promised the end of faith with its replacement by the new theory
or invention. When things were sorted out with time and experience, it turns out that the cure-all theory or invention itself was
not the final answer.

"What modern Christians find it hardest to remember," Lewis
wrote in the last essay, "is that the whole life of humanity in this
world is also temporary, temporal, provisional." The human race,

moreover, comes into being and departs from it, not all at once but one at a time. Obviously, we could conceive "the world's last night" and mankind's destiny in it to be unrelated. Indeed, this separation would be necessary if we held that the origin of the world is simply chance, with no further meaning.

We might also imagine that somewhere in the universe there is a huge sidereal object that is on a course that will eventually crash into earth, leaving nothing but ashes. Or the sun will burn out. Nonetheless, the world's last night usually implies some relationship existing between the human race itself and its intelligent origin.

We hear a good deal of talk from what are sometimes called the "earth sciences." They tell us that our real task is to hand on this planet to later generations. On this basis, we have all sorts of laws about the conservation of everything from alpacas to zinnias, from saving the forests to saving the oceans. A new morality has developed that judges us not in terms of our sins or our final personal end but in terms of what we hand down to future ages, about whom, in fact, we know nothing. Said Lewis:

> The idea which here shuts out the Second Coming from our minds, the idea of the world slowly ripening to perfection, is a myth, not a generalization from experience.... It distracts us from our real duties and our real interest. It is our attempt to guess the plot of a drama in which we are the characters. (104)

This approach attempts to play off the last men who do not exist against all those who went before and who did exist.

But a good deal of the human race has already died, maybe as many as ninety to one hundred billion of our kind. How many more to expect, we know not. Those who died before us left enough for the seven billion of us living now to prosper. As to resources, we tend to forget that resources are not just things but ideas. It seems odd, in any case, to be worried about some future last night or day, unless we think that we will be there or that the only people that count are those still alive at this last night, whenever it falls. This view seems to make the lives of those who live now or who have gone before us relatively meaningless. They have no meaning in themselves. Our only meaning is that we knowingly or unknowingly pass something down to the last men.

We need to remember, Lewis tells us, "that what may be upon us at any moment is not merely an End but a Judgment." Lewis thus puts together the two notions of End or Last Day and Judgment, that is, following Plato, an accounting for our deeds, not at some future ending but at our ending, not forgetting that our ending falls into the order of the whole of mankind that is implied in the world's last night.

> Some moderns talk as though duties to posterity were the only duties we have. I can imagine no man who will look with more horror on the End than a conscientious revolutionary who has been, in a sense sincerely, justifying cruelties and injustices inflicted on millions of his contemporaries by the benefits which he hopes to confer on future generations: generations, who now, as one terrible moment reveals to him, were never going to exist. (111)

We do not really know if there will be "future" generations, or how many, or their level of life or technology. We merely project a present theory on the future and force the world to live by it, whether it is true or not.

So in this context, the "world's last night" also serves to rescue, in Lewis's view, the very dignity of each person who has lived on this planet by taking his life, as lived, seriously enough to be judged and judged as, in fact, belonging to that drama or plan that is inherent in our cosmos and its relation to man.

> We shall not only believe but we shall know, know beyond doubt in every fiber of our appalled or delighted being, that as the Judge has said, so we are.... We shall perhaps even realize that in some dim fashion we could have known it all along. We shall know and all creation will know too; our ancestors, our parents, our wives or husbands, our children. The unanswerable and (by then) self-evident truth about each will be known to all. (113)

"The world's last night," as I said, provokes.

Lewis's conclusion is very Platonic. Plato was concerned that the world was made in vain if all the crimes committed in this world were not punished and all the good deeds unrequited. This is what the "world's last night" is about. It is the revelational response to Plato's concern. "The self-evident truth about each will be known to all."

Evidently, we are already present at the "world's last night." We are not tools for some ideological myth of perfection down the ages that may never happen.

Chapter 52

⌒

The Immaculate Conception[65]

Catholicism is an adventuresome religion, not designed for dullards, sissies, or the fainthearted. Actually, it is not a "religion" at all. Religion is about what obliges men to God insofar as they can figure it out with their reason. Religion is a form of "justice." It differs from justice because we cannot figure out exactly what we "owe" to God.

God does not "need" anything from us. Imagine a "god" that needs us to give it something! Yet, the best things are beyond "owing." No one who is given something is complete without acknowledging the gift. We human beings are even given what we are. Our very being is a gift to us. Indeed, we are gifts to one another.

Revelation is what God has told us about Himself. The only way we know how to relate to God is if God Himself informs us. "I am the way, the truth, and the life." Catholicism is based on a fact. God did inform us about Himself and about ourselves. We do not deal with a human invention, but a divine intervention.

---

[65] Published in *The Catholic Thing*, December 8, 2009.

The Reason for the Seasons

Only after the event of the Incarnation happened can we further try to figure out what it means. And we do try. Faith does seek reason, a reason that is actively reasoning. The doctrine of the Immaculate Conception of Mary, officially defined by Pius IX on December 8, 1854, is part of this seeking understanding.

Pope Pius IX wrote 155 years ago that Mary was preserved from original sin through the merits of her Son, "Jesus Christ, the Savior of the Human Race." Once we understand what the Incarnation is, this teaching about Mary's beginning makes perfectly good sense. But I doubt if Joachim, at the birth of his daughter, Mary, said to his wife, Anna: "Look, dear, she is without original sin!" Yet, one suspects that from the beginning, both parents knew that something hovered about this child of theirs.

Theology is what we can figure out using our minds about what is revealed. God informed us, as it were, that He was not a mother, but that He had a mother. At first sight, these affirmations will sound confusing if not preposterous. But we are given information that we might think about it. Usually, if we are persistent, we come up with something that for the good of our very being is worth knowing.

The Church did not first speculate about Mary and then turn to figure out who this Son of hers was. It began with the Son and worked its intellectual way backward to what His mother was and is. "Hail, Mary, full of grace": hints about her were found along the way.

In the readings for the Mass of the Immaculate Conception, we find these hints. We recall Eve and the Fall, the promise of redemption. To the Ephesians, Paul says: "Before the world was made, He chose us, chose us in Christ" (see Eph. 1:4).

In the Gospel, Mary is told "not to be afraid." And she isn't. She has "found favor"; she will "bear a Son who will be called the Son of the Most High." At this point, she tells the angel to hold up. "How can this be?"

This young woman wants the facts.

Gabriel explains.

Once she understands, Mary replies: "Let it be done unto me according to your word." And so it is. Even though she lived in an obscure town, the whole future of the world depended on her response. Whether acknowledged or not, the very being of the human race depended on the response of this young woman.

The Incarnation of the Son of God had to come from within our kind. It depended on the free response of this Mary. No wonder she herself was, as they came to say, conceived without original sin.

In the Breviary for the Immaculate Conception, the second reading is from St. Anselm, the great English bishop: "Blessed Lady, sky and stars, earth and rivers, day and night—everything that is subject to the power or use of man—rejoice that through you they are in some sense restored to their lost beauty and are endowed with inexpressible new grace."

We still find those who maintain that Catholics "worship" Mary and that *Trinity* means three gods. But we speak precisely. We do not worship Mary. We do not have three gods. Mary is the Mother of God. Her Son is the Word, the Second Person of the Trinity.

The Word, we affirm, was made "flesh" and dwelt amongst us. This is where we find Mary at Christ's birth. When he found her at Nazareth in the house of Joseph, Gabriel no doubt knew of her own "beginning."

"Blessed Lady," we rejoice that the "lost beauty" of things is restored "through you."

Conclusion

At the beginning of this book, I quoted five authors—Josef Pieper, G. K. Chesterton, Samuel Johnson, St. Augustine, and Karl Adam. My selections were not arbitrary. They are designed to anticipate, to alert the reader to the flavor and thought that goes into the various texts that follow. As the reader goes through the book, the themes found in these initial citations keep recurring.

Pieper spoke of the great "wonder" that is found in the great feasts and what they mean. Chesterton grounds Christmas in the uniqueness of the event on which it is based, its abiding relation to the family into which men are or should be born. Samuel Johnson attends the Good Friday services at St. Clement Danes Church in London. He always understood the relation between his sins and the suffering and Crucifixion of Christ. The core of Christianity takes us always to the Trinity and the relations of the Father, Son, and Spirit—this in the light of the Incarnation, the Nativity, the life and death of Christ. The destiny of the world and our place in it is an ever-present theme at the end of the Liturgical Year, the End Times. The destiny of the physical world is not related to itself but to the relation of each human being to his origin in and direction toward eternal life.

The Reason for the Seasons

Each year the liturgical cycle, in contrast to the chronological counting of days, but reflective of it, leads us through the history and nature of our salvation. No doubt, in one year, we can but touch on the riches that are found in each of the events of our redemption. As can be seen in these chapters, each year, each feast or memorial becomes a new starting point. We look again, with the new events of our own life and times, at the fact of Christ's presence in this world, during the time of Caesar Augustus.

One soon has the impression that we deal with inexhaustible things, yet things that provoke and incite us. We are aware that our own lives are given to us. We do not create them out of nothing. Yet, once we exist, we are aware that we long for some final end of our being. That longing, too, is part of what we are.

No better way can be found to make sense of our own lives than to see them in the light of the drama of God's calling us through Abraham, through the Incarnation and Redemption of Christ on the Cross, through the awareness we have that neither we ourselves nor the world itself is made fully to satisfy us, even though it can satisfy us in many good things.

The drama of our history is not that we have no end, but that the one we are freely offered is also one that we must choose. And we choose this *what we will be* by what we know and do, by what we understand to be the way that God gave us to find Him.

In the feasts that we wonder about, we are not just given a book to read, though we have that too, but a drama unfolding before us each year, a drama in which we can see ever more clearly that it is God who calls us to be what He has made us to be.

About the Author

James V. Schall, S.J., is Professor Emeritus, Georgetown University. He resides at Sacred Heart Jesuit Center, Los Gatos, California. His books include *Another Sort of Learning; On the Unseriousness of Human Affairs; Idylls & Rambles, Reasonable Pleasures*, and *The Sum Total of Human Happiness*.

Sophia Institute

Sophia Institute is a nonprofit institution that seeks to nurture the spiritual, moral, and cultural life of souls and to spread the Gospel of Christ in conformity with the authentic teachings of the Roman Catholic Church.

Sophia Institute Press fulfills this mission by offering translations, reprints, and new publications that afford readers a rich source of the enduring wisdom of mankind.

Sophia Institute also operates two popular online Catholic resources: CrisisMagazine.com and CatholicExchange.com.

Crisis Magazine provides insightful cultural analysis that arms readers with the arguments necessary for navigating the ideological and theological minefields of the day. Catholic Exchange provides world news from a Catholic perspective as well as daily devotionals and articles that will help you to grow in holiness and live a life consistent with the teachings of the Church.

In 2013, Sophia Institute launched Sophia Institute for Teachers to renew and rebuild Catholic culture through service to Catholic education. With the goal of nurturing the spiritual, moral, and cultural life of souls, and an abiding respect for the role and work of teachers, we strive to provide materials and programs that are at once enlightening to the mind and ennobling to the heart; faithful and complete, as well as useful and practical.

Sophia Institute gratefully recognizes the Solidarity Association for preserving and encouraging the growth of our apostolate over the course of many years. Without their generous and timely support, this book would not be in your hands.

www.SophiaInstitute.com
www.CatholicExchange.com
www.CrisisMagazine.com
www.SophiaInstituteforTeachers.org

Sophia Institute Press® is a registered trademark of Sophia Institute.
Sophia Institute is a tax-exempt institution as defined by the
Internal Revenue Code, Section 501(c)(3). Tax I.D. 22-2548708.